POLICE CORRUPTION

Other books in the At Issue series:

POLICE CORRUPTION

Tamara L. Roleff, *Book Editor*

Daniel Leone, *President*
Bonnie Szumski, *Publisher*
Scott Barbour, *Managing Editor*

AT ISSUE

OPPOSING VIEWPOINTS® SERIES

GREENHAVEN PRESS®

THOMSON
GALE

San Diego • Detroit • New York • San Francisco • Cleveland
New Haven, Conn. • Waterville, Maine • London • Munich

THOMSON

━━━━━✦━━━━━ ™

GALE

For more information, contact
Greenhaven Press
27500 Drake Rd.
Farmington Hills, MI 48331-3535
Or you can visit our Internet site at http://www.gale.com

LIBRARY OF CONGRESS CATALOGING-IN-PUBLICATION DATA

Police corruption / Tamara L. Roleff, book editor.
    p. cm. — (At issue)
Includes bibliographical references and index.
ISBN 0-7377-1172-8 (lib. bdg. : alk. paper) —
ISBN 0-7377-1171-X (pbk. : alk. paper)
    1. Police corruption. 2. Police corruption—United States. I. Roleff, Tamara L.,
1959– . II. At issue (San Diego, Calif.)
HV7936.C85 P65   2003
353.4'6—dc21
                                                     2002021478

Printed in the United States of America

Contents

Introduction

In the fall of 1999, Rafael Perez, a police officer in the Los Angeles Police Department's crime- and gangster-ridden Rampart Division, was arrested for stealing three kilos of cocaine that had been confiscated as evidence during an undercover drug deal. In exchange for a lighter sentence, Perez, who was assigned to the elite antigang unit known as CRASH (Community Resources Against Street Hoodlums), offered to tell investigators about other crimes he and his fellow Rampart officers had committed. The highest-profile crime Perez admitted to was shooting Javier Francisco Ovando in October 1996 and subsequently planting a gun on him to frame him for attacking him and his partner. Ovando, who was paralyzed by the shooting, was sentenced to twenty-three years in prison, but was released in September 1999 after Perez's confession. Perez also told investigators that he helped cover up two other unjustified shootings by Rampart police officers, including one incident in which the victim bled to death while police officers delayed an ambulance's arrival while they conferred on their cover story. He implicated more than seventy officers in such acts of misconduct as drug dealing, planting evidence, making false arrests, and covering up crimes they had themselves committed.

During more than fifty hours of interviews with authorities, Perez discussed how he went from a hard-charging rookie to a cynical and corrupt police officer. The first time he stole money from a suspect was in 1997 when he and his partner, Nino Durden, arrested a drug dealer. They confiscated a pound of cocaine and a pager from the dealer but kept them instead of turning them in. When the dealer's pager went off, they arranged a meeting to sell the drug, initially intending to arrest the drug buyer. According to Perez, when they arrived at the meeting site Durden said, "'Screw it, let's just sell to him.' And I completely agreed." Perez and Durden made two other sales from the confiscated cocaine and netted about $10,000. After that incident, Perez said he and Durden broke the law almost as frequently as they enforced it.

Other officers beside Perez and Durden were also actively involved in acts of misconduct and corruption. Perez told investigators about officers who crashed a party attended by gang members. One officer had the gang members drop to their knees while he walked behind them and told them what fabricated crimes he was going to charge them with. Another officer repeatedly shot a suspect with a bean bag gun for sport. One police officer rounded up a gang member he believed was responsible for slashing the tires of his patrol car, stripped him naked, and dropped him in enemy gang territory. Perez told authorities that of the fifteen officers in his squad, thirteen framed innocent people for crimes they did not commit.

Following Perez's confession, the Los Angeles district attorney's office had to reexamine thousands of cases in which the implicated officers were involved to determine if the suspects had been unfairly accused and convicted. According to Perez, "90 percent of the officers who work CRASH, and not just Rampart CRASH, falsify a lot of information. . . . It hurts me to say it, but there's a lot of crooked stuff going on in the LAPD." As a result of his allegations, more than one hundred convictions had been overturned by the end of 2001, and Los Angeles officials are expecting to pay out millions of dollars to settle lawsuits against the city.

Bernard C. Parks, chief of police for the Los Angeles Police Department (LAPD), established a Board of Inquiry to investigate Perez's allegations. According to the Board of Inquiry's March 2000 report into the Rampart area corruption scandal, there were many breakdowns in the organization that allowed the police corruption to grow and spread. Chief among the report's findings was evidence of mediocre performance by police officers throughout Los Angeles. The report claims that officers with integrity and those who were just coasting by saw that the offenses of mediocre officers were not dealt with, so they also began to allow their standards to decline. According to the report, "Rather than challenging our people to do their best, too many of our leaders are allowing mediocre performance, and, in some cases, even making excuses for it." The authors continue, "Many of these officers allowed their personal integrity to erode and their activities certainly had a contagion effect on some of those around them." Other faults that contributed to the corruption scandal were inadequate screening of new recruits and a failure to supervise officers in the field and monitor their misconduct. However, the board was insistent on pointing out that

> the Rampart corruption incident occurred because a few individuals decided to engage in blatant misconduct and, in some cases, criminal behavior. Published assertions by . . . Rafael Perez that the pressure to produce arrests caused him to become corrupt, simply ignores the fact that he was convicted of stealing narcotics so he could sell them and live the life style of a "high roller." Even the finest corruption prevention system will not stop an individual from committing a crime if he or she has the will to do so.

In addition, the Board of Inquiry found several problems in the recruiting, hiring, and training of police officers, as well as inattentive and ineffective managers and supervisors that contributed to an atmosphere conducive to police corruption.

The board discovered that four of the officers under investigation for corruption had a criminal record, problems with managing their finances, and a history of violent behavior and involvement in drugs. It also found that assignments to the Rampart Division were based on a sponsorship system in which new officers were nominated for inclusion rather than by a promotion system that awarded ability or experience. The report discussed the fact that few citizen complaints against Rampart officers were taken seriously by police supervisors and that management failed to recognize and correct officer misconduct. It concluded that many of the problems it found during its inquiry were due to the fact that police—from upper management down to patrol officers—were "failing to do their jobs with a high level of consistency and integrity."

Shortly after the Board of Inquiry released its report about the corruption scandal at Rampart, Erwin Chemerinsky, a renowned legal ethicist and professor of public interest law at the University of Southern California, prepared an analysis of the report. He begins by arguing that the corruption scandal is

> the worst scandal in the history of Los Angeles. Police officers framed innocent individuals by planting evidence and committing perjury to gain convictions. Nothing is more inimical to the rule of law than police officers, sworn to uphold the law, flouting it and using their authority to convict innocent people. Innocent men and women pleaded guilty to crimes they did not commit and were convicted by juries because of the fabricated cases against them.

He adds, "Any analysis of the Rampart scandal must begin with an appreciation of the heinous nature of what the officers did. This is conduct associated with the most repressive dictators and police states." In Chemerinsky's opinion, the Board of Inquiry minimized the seriousness and extent of the corruption and the impact it had on the community. In addition, he contends that the Board of Inquiry did not discuss the notorious "Code of Silence" in which police officers refuse to discuss or turn a blind eye to their colleagues' misconduct.

The issues raised by the Board of Inquiry and by Chemerinsky are common to all other police corruption incidents. Poor hiring practices and inadequate training and supervision are perhaps the biggest contributors to police corruption. In *Police Corruption: At Issue*, the authors examine these issues in more detail and also discuss how corruption can be prevented or detected once it occurs.

1

Overview: Ethics and Police Integrity

Stephen J. Vicchio

Stephen J. Vicchio, a professor of philosophy at the College of Notre Dame in Baltimore, Maryland, is a nationally renowned ethicist and a faculty member in the Police Executive Leadership Program at Johns Hopkins University in Baltimore, and at Johns Hopkins School of Medicine. He gave this keynote speech at the National Symposium on Police Integrity held in Washington, D.C., in July 1996.

There are two reasons why people act in a good and moral way. One is because they fear punishment if they are caught doing wrong; the second is because people want to be morally good. Police officers frequently act on the principle that people do good because they are afraid of getting caught. However, if this is true, then people, including police officers, will continue to do wrong because there will never be enough supervision to catch them doing wrong. This is especially true for police officers, who have little fear of being caught. People with integrity—those who do good— are committed to a stable set of core virtues. Values essential for police officers with professional integrity are prudence, trust, courage, honesty, justice, responsibility, and an obliteration of self-interest to serve the public good. Police officers should demonstrate more integrity than the general population.

> We should therefore examine whether we should act in this way or not, as not only now, but at all times.
>
> —Plato
>
> If he really does not think there is no distinction between virtue and vice, why sir, when he leaves the house, let us count the spoons.
>
> —Samuel Johnson, Letters

There is an old saying that "philosophers bake no bread." What this expression is supposed to mean, I gather, is that philosophers spend a good deal of time minding other people's business while not spending

From "Ethics and Police Integrity," by Stephen J. Vicchio, *Police Integrity: Public Service with Honor*, January 1997.

nearly enough on their own. Working entirely in this spirit, the spirit of an interloper, in this paper I wish to talk about three issues—issues vital to the success of this conference and, ultimately, to the success of police organizations throughout the country. First, I wish to sketch out in a brief way what I see as the component parts of the concept of integrity. Second, I would like to spend a little time exploring what the latest social scientific research and common sense have to say about whether integrity can be taught. And, finally, I will end with some observations on the question of whether integrity can be measured in professional contexts such as police work. At the very end, if I might be so bold, I will also make some general recommendations about additional questions and approaches that might be helpful in discussing the issue of police integrity. I will begin, however, with a short take from Plato's *Republic*.

In this section [Book II] of the *Republic,* Socrates discusses with his friend Glaucon what it means to act in a morally responsible way. Glaucon puts forth a theory that is not all that far from a general view of the issue that many hold in this country. In essence, Glaucon says that we do good because we risk punishment if we do wrong. Thus, we accept certain limitations on our freedom because we are afraid of being caught. So justice, in Glaucon's view, is a kind of arrangement (like traffic lights or stop signs) that is not intrinsically good or valuable but put into place to avoid harm.

In the course of their discussion, Glaucon and Socrates allude to an old Greek story, "The Ring of Gyges." The wearer of the ring was rendered invisible, though he or she could still affect the material world as visible bodies do. In the course of the tale, the shepherd Gyges is given the ring, and he uses it without fear of reprisal. Indeed, he uses it to kill the king of Lydia and later to rape the queen.

Glaucon argues that anyone in the shepherd's position would be foolish not to take full advantage of the power of the ring. In essence, it gives the wearer the ability to do wrong with impunity. Glaucon then goes on to suggest that justice is nothing more than a series of checks, a system of preventive devices. But if we possessed the ring of Gyges, there would be no good reason for doing the good. In the remainder of the *Republic,* Socrates attempts to counter Glaucon's view by suggesting that the citizens of a good society would act justly because they knew and appreciated the moral good and not merely because they were afraid of getting caught.

No supervision of police officers working with the public, no matter how thorough and conscientious, can keep bad cops from doing bad things.

There are several reasons why I begin with Plato's story. It is best, I think, to look at "The Ring of Gyges" as a cautionary tale, for it seems to me, for better or worse, the police officers in this country, at least when they are working on the street, often are possessors of the ring of Gyges. No supervision of police officers working with the public, no matter how thorough and conscientious, can keep bad cops from doing bad things. There simply are too many police officers and too few supervisors. Like it or not, the police in this country are possessors of the ring of Gyges.

A second realization to be made from Plato's tale is that police departments in this country often operate as if Glaucon's view of justice is the proper one—that we do the good out of fear, a level that developmental psychologists tell us is the lowest common denominator in the moral equation. If we put these two points together, that there will never be enough supervision to catch everyone and that good behavior on the job is motivated by fear, we should see that they are contradictory. If there is not enough supervision, then the bad cop will not be afraid. If we add a third element, that the bad cop always makes the news, then we have a recipe for disaster.

Public trust in the police

One of the major repercussions of the confluence of these three elements, (1) Glaucon's view of virtue, (2) there will never be enough supervisors to catch everyone, and (3) the bad cop always makes the news, is that we see over the past two decades in America an erosion of public confidence in public officials and their institutions. Consider, for example, the following tables of Americans' ratings of their confidence in various professionals. In this study 100 Americans were asked to rank the moral confidence/trust they have in the following professionals to do the right thing. (Position 1 is most trusted, position 12 is least trusted of those professions listed.)

1980	1995
1. pharmacist	1. firefighter
2. clergy	2. pharmacist
3. firefighter	3. teacher
4. teacher	4. dentist
5. police officer	5. clergy
6. doctor	6. stock broker
7. dentist	7. doctor
8. accountant	8. accountant
9. stock broker	9. funeral director
10. lawyer	10. police officer
11. funeral director	11. lawyer
12. politician	12. politician

In this study, trust in police officers recorded the largest drop from 1980 to 1995 (5 spaces), followed by the clergy (3), doctors (1), and lawyers (1), though lawyers simply moved from 10th position to 11th.

Another disturbing element to these findings is that although there was no significant difference between men and women respondents, there was a very big difference between African-American and white respondents. Among blacks, "police officer" had the 9th position in 1980 and the 11th position in 1995, just ahead of "politician."

One major conclusion we can make from this study and from other like studies from around the country is that the public thinks police departments have an integrity problem, even if the police themselves do not.

What complicates this issue still further is that in departments where corruption appears to be low and where citizen complaints are minimal, we assume that our officers on the job are people of integrity. Sometimes this is a faulty assumption, particularly if the motivation to do the right thing comes from fear of punishment. Often in professional contexts in this country we think of integrity as our ability to refrain from certain activities. But, clearly, if the concept is to mean something more than what Glaucon suggests, it must involve higher levels of thinking and feeling on the part of police officers.

The public thinks police departments have an integrity problem, even if the police themselves do not.

If we believe that community policing is the most effective way to protect and to serve the public, and then we put officers who operate from the fear of punishment in more direct contact with the community, then the community will not find officers of integrity but, rather, people who know the rules and regulations and keep them simply because they are afraid of getting caught. [Bob Trojanowicz defines community policing as "a philosophy of full-service, personalized policing where the same officer patrols and works in the same area on a permanent basis . . . working in a proactive partnership with citizens to identify and solve problems."]

If this conference has some major goals, it seems to me, they should include these: How do we define integrity? How do we identify it in police officers? How do we make sure that the police officers we involve in community policing efforts are people of character and integrity? If we do not answer these core questions, then a conference like this is useless, indeed perhaps worse than useless, because we have pretended to get something done. Pretending to get something done in any profession is always dangerous. Let us then try to make some headway in our first question: What do we mean by the concept of integrity?

The concept of integrity

The first thing to say about the concept of integrity is that we often use organic or spatial metaphors to explain it. This, of course, hints at the etymological origins of the word integritas, "whole or complete." But when we go beyond the metaphors, it is not so easy to articulate what we mean when we say that a person possesses integrity.

Martin Benjamin, in a helpful book called *Splitting the Difference: Compromise and Integrity in Ethics and Politics,* identifies five psychological types lacking in integrity. The first he calls the *moral chameleon.* Benjamin describes the type this way:

> Anxious to accommodate others and temperamentally indisposed to moral controversy and disagreement, the moral chameleon is quick to modify or abandon previously avowed principles. . . . Apart from a commitment to accommodation, the moral chameleon has little in the way of core values. . . . The moral chameleon bears careful watching. If placed in a situation where retaining her principles requires resisting social pressure, she is likely to betray others as she betrays herself.

Benjamin's second type, the *moral opportunist,* is similar to the moral chameleon in that his values are ever-changing. But where the moral chameleon tries to avoid conflict, the moral opportunist places primary value on his own short-term self-interest. While the moral chameleon's motto might be "above all, get along," the moral opportunist's is "above all, get ahead."

The *moral hypocrite* is a third type lacking in integrity. "The hypocrite," writes Gabriele Taylor, "pretends to live by certain standards when in fact he does not." The hypocrite has one set of virtues for public consumption, and another set he actually has as a moral code. The lack of integrity comes in that the hypocrite pretends that the code is different than what it actually is.

Benjamin's fourth type, the *morally weak-willed,* has a reasonably coherent set of core virtues, but they usually lack the courage to act on them. They are unlike the moral chameleon in that they know what the good is, they simply lack the courage to do it. Benjamin's final type, the *moral self-deceivers,* have at their core a basic contradiction. They think of themselves as acting on a set of core principles, while in fact they do not. To resolve this conflict, and at the same time to preserve their idealized view of themselves, they deceive themselves about what they are doing.

The police officer of integrity habitually will exhibit traits of character that make clear the goals of protection and service.

By looking at these five types, we immediately see what integrity does not look like. But if we look a little closer, we also may get some hints about a proper understanding of the concept. First, a person of integrity has a reasonably coherent and relatively stable set of core moral virtues. And second, the person's acts and speech tend to reflect those principles. Individual integrity, then, requires that one's words and actions should be of a piece, and they should reflect a set of core virtues to which one is freely and genuinely committed.

But what ought these virtues to be? The answer to that question may differ in different professional contexts, but integrity in the context of police work should amount to the sum of the virtues required to bring about the general goals of protection and service to the public. In short, professional virtue should always bring about the moral goals of the professional organization in question. A list of the virtues of a good cop, then, ought to tell us something important about why police departments exist. Professional integrity, then, in any professional context, is the integrated collection of virtues that brings about the goals of the profession. Presumably, in police organizations those major goals are connected to protection of and service to the public.

A list of core virtues

Lists of professional virtues are difficult, if not foolish, to compose, particularly if an interloper is doing the compiling. The following list is, of course, by no means complete. Rather, I consider it to be essential to the purposes of police organizations. These virtues, in other words, must be required by police officers if the goals of the organization are to be met. These virtues are not listed here in any order.

- Prudence. Practical wisdom, the virtue of deliberation and discernment. The ability to unscramble apparent conflicts between virtues while deciding what action (or refraining from action) is best in a given situation.
- Trust. This virtue is entailed by the three primary relationships of the police officer: the citizen-officer relationship, the officer-officer relationship, and the officer-supervisor relationship. Trust ought to engender loyalty and truthfulness in these three contexts.
- Effacement of self-interests. Given the "exploitability" of citizens, self-effacement is important. Without it, citizens can become a means to advance the police officer's power, prestige, or profit, or a means for advancing goals of the department other than those to protect and to serve.
- Courage. As Aristotle suggests, this virtue is a golden mean between two extremes: cowardice and foolhardiness. There are many professions—surgery and police work, to name two—where the difference between courage and foolhardiness is extremely important.
- Intellectual honesty. Acknowledging when one does not know something and being humble enough to admit ignorance is an important virtue in any professional context. The lack of this virtue in police work can be very dangerous.
- Justice. We normally think of justice as giving the individual what he or she is due. But taking the virtue of justice in a police context sometimes requires the removal of justice's blindfold and adjusting what is owed to a particular citizen, even when those needs do not fit the definition of what is strictly owed.
- Responsibility. Again, Aristotle suggests that a person who exhibits responsibility is one who intends to do the right thing, has a clear understanding of what the right thing is, and is fully cognizant of other alternatives that might be taken. More importantly, a person of integrity is one who does not attempt to evade responsibility by finding excuses for poor performance or bad judgment.

The fear of punishment has rarely been enough to change habitual behavior.

At a minimum, then, these seven virtues are required for integrity because they are required as well by the general goals of police organizations. There are probably other virtues I have missed, but most others will be variants of these seven. In short, a police officer who exhibits integrity is a person who has successfully integrated these seven virtues so that they become a whole greater than the parts. The police officer of integrity habitually will exhibit traits of character that make clear the goals of protection and service.

In The Johns Hopkins Police Executive Leadership Program, we are planning a study that will attempt to identify exemplary police officers. We hope to determine whether the virtues we have listed above, as well as some others, are consistently found among the best of our police officers. Additionally, we hope to analyze the relationship of these virtues to performance evaluations, commendations, citizen complaints, and other variables and also to ask them for practical advice about how and why they have remained good cops.

Can integrity be taught?

Needless to say, this is a second important question that should be at the top of our research agenda. If one looks at what evidence is now available from social scientific literature, the answer to our question seems to be "yes" and "no." Since most researchers agree that the practice of virtue—the component parts of integrity—is a habitual activity, it must be learned and reinforced. Other evidence suggests that the most effective time to teach virtue is early on, so the "yes" part of our answer is that children in stable, loving homes who regularly have the requisite virtues modeled for them are the most successful people at developing a track record for integrity.

The "no" part of the answer comes with the realization that most evidence about problems with integrity suggest that they, too, are habitual problems. By and large, people who habitually have trouble in school with behavioral problems become adults who have the same problems. This is not to say that people's behaviors cannot change. But change always comes when the person has a clear goal and incentive for changing. The fear of punishment has rarely been enough to change habitual behavior.

These findings clearly should have some important ramifications for the way we go about recruiting and testing police officers. Testing instruments need to be better than they are now. Longitudinal studies need to be completed that show us how well we have done in the past and the present in recruiting people who will grow to be police officers of integrity. This is one of the goals of the Hopkins study I alluded to earlier.

One other area of inquiry worth pursuing is to track the relationship of the kind and extent of ethics training in police academies to the performance of those recruits as police officers. My initial sense is that the more extensive the training, the clearer the effect will be, though the social scientific evidence on the relationship of academic ethics training and moral behavior, at least at this point, is ambiguous. One element about academy ethics training is clear: if it is to be effective, it needs to be rigorous and it needs to emphasize critical thinking skills, reasoning skills, reasoning ability, and problem-solving techniques. In short, it needs to be the right blend of the theoretical and the practical.

Can integrity be measured?

The answer to this question in the general area of professional activity is that we do not know. If we measure police integrity the way State medical organizations measure the integrity of physicians or the way State judicial review boards measure the integrity of lawyers, we will not be successful. Historically, these organizations try to determine what their members have been successful in avoiding. Integrity in these contexts is seen as not leaving a sponge in a patient's abdominal cavity or not having conflicts of interest. In short, these governing bodies look to see if the doctor or lawyer has followed the rules and regulations and has avoided doing wrong. But avoiding wrong behavior is not the same as having integrity, any more than simply avoiding bad notes will get a singer to Carnegie Hall.

If we are to be successful in measuring police integrity, we must find measuring tools that not only enable us to determine that police officers effectively avoid certain behaviors but that they also regularly practice prudence, courage, justice, honesty, trust, self-effacement, and responsibility.

One way to begin this task is first to refine the definition and identification of the virtues that go into making a police officer of integrity. If we have missed the boat in identifying what we see as the core virtues, we will know soon enough. A second item that must be put on our list of things to do is the development of an agenda—a national mission statement, if you will—that says in a broad way what the moral purposes are of police organizations. All definitions of virtue and integrity, Aristotle forcefully argues, only make sense in the context of what he calls telos, the larger reason or purpose in which those virtues are placed. What we want a department to be ultimately should tell us a great deal about what we want our officers to do.

If we are going to think of ourselves as a profession, then we must assume the level of responsibility that a professional life entails. The profession ought to require more from its members than we expect from the general population.

2

An Examination of Police Corruption

Frank L. Perry

Frank L. Perry, the former chief of the Ethics Unit, Office of Professional Responsibility, at the FBI Academy in Quantico, Virginia, is head of the FBI agency in Raleigh, North Carolina.

Most studies of police corruption are beginning to reject the "bad apple" theory—that corrupt officers are only a few rotten apples in the barrel. Instead, they are beginning to examine the "barrel"—the individual police department—for signs that corruption is allowed, encouraged, or ignored. Police departments must ensure that only fully qualified applicants who demonstrate integrity are selected to become police officers. To prevent corruption, police officers should be frequently assigned new roles or to different departments, especially those officers who work in positions that are more prone to corruption, such as vice squads or drug units. In addition, police officers should be held to a higher standard of conduct than ordinary citizens, and the standards should be raised as an officer progresses through the ranks.

In the last two decades, research and commentary regarding the causes and effects of law enforcement corruption have intensified and diversified. Efforts in Australia, Canada, Great Britain, and the United States have effectively identified symptoms and remedies in those countries, as emerging democracies in Africa, Eastern Europe, and the Pacific Rim face the more immediate and stark realities of self-governance and the police role. Comparative reviews of problems and best practices, as well as academic research, suggest that corruption follows certain predictable routes and that precursory signs occur prior to any actual quid pro quo corrupt activity.

Three organizational failures can foster a resentful, cynical, and demoralized work force leading to individual and collective acts of corruption. These failures are: little or ineffective discipline and deselection of trainees (a commitment to fairly but firmly graduate only those individuals who truly demonstrate performance and integrity standards); igno-

From "Repairing Broken Windows: Preventing Corruption Within Our Ranks," by Frank L. Perry, *FBI Bulletin,* February 2001.

rance of the nature and effects of the goal-gradient phenomenon (the farther away individuals remain from their goal, the less the tendency to remain passionately interested in its attainment); and the allowance of a double standard within the organization, thereby decreasing moral accountability as professional responsibility increases. All of these factors represent instances of what sociologists have referred to for many years as the "broken window theory"—if enough broken windows in a neighborhood go unattended, the neighborhood falls into a moral and material malaise. Law enforcement applications of this theory are addressed rarely.

Understanding corruption

Corruption can include an abuse of position, although not all abuses of position constitute corrupt acts. Committing a criminal act under color of law represents one example of corruption, while using one's law enforcement position for a *de minimus,* or insignificant, private gain may not necessarily rise to what reasonable persons will call a corrupt act, though it may be corrupting. All self-interested or potentially corrupt acts are not completely corrupt. In fact, these acts can constitute police deviance, which best captures the nature of the precursory signs of corruption, as opposed to actual corruption.

Precursory signs, or instances of police deviance, may be agency-specific, or generic and found in law enforcement as a profession. Unprofessional on- and off-duty misconduct, isolated instances of misuse of position, improper relationships with informants or criminals, sexual harassment, disparaging racial or sexual comments, embellished/falsified reporting, time and attendance abuse, insubordination, nepotism, cronyism, and noncriminal unauthorized disclosure of information all represent precursory signs of police deviance that inspection and internal affairs components must monitor. When agencies determine a trend of increasing frequency and egregiousness of such deviance, they must take steps before classic or quid pro quo corruption occurs. An organization with an increase in such deviance becomes a "rotten barrel," even without completely "rotten apples."

Literature on the rotten-barrel concept has become more sophisticated. One study, [quoting former New York Police Commissioner Patrick Murphy,] surmises that most of the major inquiries into police corruption reject the "bad-apple" theory: "The rotten-apple theory won't work any longer. Corrupt police officers are not natural-born criminals, nor morally wicked men, constitutionally different from their honest colleagues. The task of corruption control is to examine the barrel, not just the apples, the organization, not just the individual in it, because corrupt police are made, not born."

How, then, can agencies examine the barrel? They must analyze the increasing frequency and egregiousness of precursory signs, then assess their department's training. Agencies must not treat deselection expressly or implicitly as a negative or detrimental policy. No trainee has a right to become a law enforcement officer, although all qualified persons have an equal right to compete for such an assignment. Personnel, applicant, or recruitment officers within police agencies cannot predict who will meet all suitability and trustworthiness standards prior to the training setting.

Therefore, the training components must make this determination with an overriding focus on the agency's mission, image, and efficacy, while maintaining a respect-of-persons principle. This means deselection—a commitment to fairly but firmly graduate only those who truly demonstrate performance and integrity standards. Organizational laziness in this regard is detrimental to the agency and to the community it protects. Once immersed in the weighty discretion and low visibility of law enforcement culture, those who do not meet minimal suitability and trustworthiness standards will contribute invariably to the frequency of the precursory signs. The practical conclusion drawn from recent research [by John Kleinig] is that, "in order to distance oneself morally from serious corruption, it is important not to engage in any corruption, albeit corruption of an apparently trivial kind. . . . Once a certain practice is accepted, people are likely to go on to accept other practices that are increasingly unacceptable."

Failure to impartially deselect trainees based upon suitability and trustworthiness standards eventually determines the organizational grade of the infamous slippery slope. The higher the performance and integrity standards for successful completion of the training program, the greater the angle from actual performance and moral peak to potential failure. Metaphorically, the organizational culture will help prevent individual slide because the ethical and performance slope is so steep and the incremental slide more obvious and preventive. Conversely, the more gradual the slope, the less the perception of moral and administrative slide.

Corruption can include an abuse of position, although not all abuses of position constitute corrupt acts.

Additionally, law enforcement agencies must understand and confront the goal-gradient phenomenon, a facet of human behavior most relevant to law enforcement work and culture. In general, the closer individuals get to their goal, the faster they run (a race), the harder they try (a career), or the more interest they show (working late the night before a vacation). Applied to law enforcement, the goal-gradient phenomenon suggests that the midpoint in an officer's career can present a danger zone for malaise, resentment, cynicism, or just plain boredom. Such attitudes fuel precursory corruption or police deviance, if not actual corruption. Most professionals in any field of endeavor can deal with and overcome the "too late to quit and too early to retire" syndrome successfully, but when burdened with the rigors of the very nature of law enforcement, such as high discretion, low visibility, and criminal element interaction, and weighed down further by an agency culture of poor recruitment, ineffective training, and inept internal controls, then the goal-gradient phenomenon can become fatal—to a career and to an organization.

Preventing corruption

How can law enforcement agencies counter this tendency of human nature? First, agencies should consider frequent assignment moves, especially from and to the areas of policing more prone to corruption. Geographical and intradivisional reassignments prevent stagnation, broaden experience, and preempt lasting effects of deleterious associations—albeit perhaps at the expense of deepening expertise in a single area.

Corrupt police officers are not natural-born criminals, nor morally wicked men, constitutionally different from their honest colleagues.

Second, agencies should "feed the eagles." One police corruption investigation, [discussed by Tim Newburn,] "perhaps best known for its distinction between 'grass eaters' and 'meat eaters,' also included a third category: the 'birds.' The birds were the officers who flew above the corruption, seeking safety in the safe and rarified air of administrative positions." The birds fly above corruption or deviance, but sometimes they also confront it. Certainly, these birds who aspire for management ranks can, to further the analogy, become "eagles." The eagle confronts corruption, soars to perform duties in the most noble fashion possible, and, thereby, raises the organization's dignity and effectiveness. Thus, agencies should select, nurture, and promote individuals who demonstrate these attributes early.

Efforts to counter the goal gradient should include positive reinforcement. Individuals relish fair and honest praise, commendation, and recognition. Agencies should do the same for all of their employees as long as flattery, political gain, or gratuitous self-promotion are not intended. True professionals respect each other, and the goal gradient simply will not take hold where a culture of support, commonality, respect of persons, and appreciation of performance exists.

Third, the double standard must die. [According to Edwin J. Delattre,] "Those who serve the public must be held to a higher standard of honesty and care for the public good than the general citizenry. . . . A higher standard is not a double standard. Persons accepting positions of public trust take on new obligations and are free not to accept them if they do not want to live up to the higher standard." Beginning a career in law enforcement—perhaps the most entrusting and powerful service for the public good—entails a higher standard of conduct and calling for the trainee. Certainly, this reasoning should continue up through and to the command or executive management level. Who could argue that with increasing rank within a law enforcement agency comes either diminished or even the same obligation to the public good as that of a support employee, patrol officer, or street investigator? If the premise that individuals accepting positions of public trust take on new obligations, then it follows that the higher the position, the higher the standard. Birds must fly, but they also must land. Noble eagles do not hide in the underbrush of hidden agendas or attempts at cover-up and cronyism. Administrators must hold law enforcement eagles more accountable for their actions because they see more, know more, have more visibility, receive more pay, and must make responsible decisions for the sake of the agency's mission and, correspondingly, for the public good. Law enforcement agencies

most resistant to corruption remove temptation, increase the fear of detection, and emphasize managerial responsibility. Moreover, leadership
on the part of these agencies' senior officers consists of their willingness,
[as M. Punch writes,] to "state explicitly and openly that . . . they will per-
sonally serve as role models for integrity."

The benefits of preventing corruption lie in stark contrast to the contempt, cynicism, and resentment generated within an organization—and
for an organization as viewed by the taxpayer—when it winks at misconduct, whether precursory, deviant, corrupt, or criminal, on the part of
management. As some researchers emphasize, increasing managerial
moral responsibility and accountability builds institutional pride. It dies
when a policy creates a double standard or when favoritism, cronyism, or
career aggrandizement develop it.

Therefore, internal controls must remain firm, fair, and fast, as well
as forthright. Even an appearance of management protecting its own in
substantiated cases of misconduct will not only cause forfeiture of an
agency's internal police powers, but will ruin the agency itself.

Avoiding deselection, ignoring the goal gradient, and promoting or
permitting a double standard of internal controls can result in corruption
in law enforcement agencies. Internal affairs and ethics components
within law enforcement agencies, therefore, must remain, [according to
Newburn,] "vigilant and skeptical." Neither attribute is akin to cynicism or
arrogance, and neither vigilance nor skepticism need be born of zealots.
Monitoring human conduct within law enforcement agencies—themselves designed to monitor human conduct writ large—must be done
with uncompromising care for human dignity, while carefully maintaining and enhancing the mission of the agency.

3

Police Culture Encourages Corruption

Anthony V. Bouza

Anthony V. Bouza, a former chief of police in Minneapolis and comman-der of the Bronx police force, has written several books about policing.

Police officers belong to a close-knit fraternity that expects mem-bers to conform. New recruits learn that they must back up other police officers no matter what the circumstances; officers who at-tempt to point out corruption, lies, abuse of authority, or other acts of wrong-doing are ostracized, harassed, and condemned by their colleagues. Many police officers refuse to provide back-up for whistle-blowers, which leaves them facing dangerous situations alone. While most officers are honest, hardworking, and respon-sible, the taint of corruption touches them all, whether they are willing participants or not. All officers realize they must participate in the Code of Silence—by either claiming ignorance of or else out-right supporting another officer's criminal acts—if they are to re-main members in good standing with the police fraternity.

I t is kind of remarkable how cops take a callow youth and transform him into a compliant member of the cult.

It starts with graduation from a police academy that basically serves as an apprenticeship for the development of the essential skills needed to function. Once acquired, the acolyte is turned over to a "hairbag" (in the NYPD [New York Police Department], a wizened pro) to teach him the ropes.

Acculturation invariably starts with a slogan that rarely varies by a syllable, "Forget about the bullshit they taught you at the academy, kid; this is the real world." Next comes an introduction into a universe whose existence is not suspected—not even by the recruit. The values are trans-mitted and reinforced, in an endless series of proddings, hints, examples, and nods.

"Stand-up guys," who protect the brethren, keep quiet, and back you up, are proudly pointed out; and pariahs among the force come in all shapes, sizes, and levels of opprobrium, sharing only the visceral contempt of their associates.

It's okay to be a little weird. Deviance can be tolerated, if it doesn't threaten the group.

"Rats" are scorned, shunned, excluded, condemned, harassed, and, almost invariably, cast out. No back-up for them. They literally find cheese in their lockers. Unwanted items are delivered to their homes. The phone rings at all hours—followed by menacing silences, anonymous imprecations, or surprisingly inventive epithets. The police radio crackles with invective. The message is eloquent and pervasive.

Remarkably, the brass joins in.

It is kind of remarkable how cops take a callow youth and transform him into a compliant member of the cult.

It soon becomes clear that, just as threats to authority are put down with swift and sure punishments (e.g., uniform violations such as wearing some unallowed item or doffing a hat, or challenging a superior, or other forms of truculence), violations against group cohesion and protection, for whatever motive, are snuffed out quickly even when—actually, especially when—they carry the offensive odor of reform or attempts to uncover wrongdoing in the ranks.

The Mafia never enforced its code of blood-sworn *omerta* with the ferocity, efficacy, and enthusiasm the police bring to the Blue Code of Silence.

Stand-up guys and gals have balls. This includes silence or support. It does not include contradiction or exposure.

Cops are physically brave. Cowardice is an unthinkable option and an unmentionable word. It is as if it is so unacceptable as to be unacknowledged as a possibility. In thirty-six years in that world, I saw only one certifiable instance of cowardice—when a cop abandoned a partner in a close-encounter gun battle, and was fired.

Very often the "thumpers," the quick-fisted, violent cop leaders on the street, are the first through the door, the first to show up to give blood to a fallen mate, the loudest in asserting group interests, and the untitled vanguard setting the tone within the ranks. They sometimes achieve titles, too, but usually in union posts.

We are accustomed to equating courage with nobility but, in the police world, the bravest are often the most brutal. And, because of their willing immersion in the sometimes awful realities of policing, they are widely admired by others in the ranks. Ask any cop to define a "great cop" and, if he or she gives you an honest answer, it will be laced with adjectives that, to an uninitiated ear, might prove borderline cruel or even shockingly aggressive.

"Active cops," or the cops who make the most collars and get the most action on the street, often have records marked by troubling signposts of brutality, productive arrest and citation records, and medals for heroism. These cops communicate a mixed and even incomprehensible message to the civilian world. They can be either heroes or sadists—or both.

It has been said that policing offers a ringside seat on the greatest show on earth.

What is that show?

It is the human animal in dishabille—drunk, violent, battered or battering, sexually exposed (in such resplendent variety as to impoverish the imagination), and at his worst, lowest, meanest, most vulnerable, and revealing. Policing provides a fascinating look at the real animal beneath the patina of civilization we conceitedly assume to be our true nature. The cops are society's charnel house cleaners and are privy to *our* goriest secrets.

Cops come into secret knowledge by being admitted into our secret acts. Cops don't bother to speculate whether this or that person could possibly kill another; they see that, rubbed hard enough, anyone could—and often does—kill.

Cops learn that psychos are dangerous and frequently possessed of superhuman strength fueled by manic-driven adrenaline rushes—and the power of even small, slight people under its influence can reach incredible levels. When they try explaining this they are usually met with uncomprehending stares. The cops think, Well, fine, you go and respond to the knife-wielding maniac in the corridor and I'll go home. But they can't.

Cops know that fans at a ballpark can turn into rioters, and parade watchers can transform into manhandlers of women.

So they learn to act, cover their asses, back each other up, and say nothing.

Cynicism

The underbelly of the human beast reveals not only insights that produce profound cynicism, but oftentimes even black humor. The enduring hallmark of every cop's character is, in fact, the very antithesis of the contemptible naïf—cynicism. There are many strange birds in the police world, but no naive turkeys. There have been learned studies of police cynicism, which is the one characteristic unfailingly transmitted by the experience of policing.

[Cops] learn to act, cover their asses, back each other up, and say nothing.

Cops, by learning just how very thin the veneer of civilization is over every human's psychic skin, know what that animal is capable of. Cops come in all shapes, sizes, and attitudes—in a wild profusion of varieties—but they share one quality: the sobering knowledge of human possibilities, and this cannot be observed without engendering a profound skepticism, caution, or suspicion. This soon, unfortunately, changes into cynicism.

Cynicism, in this hard world, frequently finds its expressions in black humor that may feature body parts, sexual functions, or other rough passages.

Young cops excitedly share their thrilling discoveries with those near to them and are silently appalled when they discover that "civilians" don't get it. Even loved ones are outsiders. Their laughter comes, if at all, in the wrong places. The flow of questions reveals the gap between their worlds, and the judgments offered can be harsh and unexpected.

Quickly, a cop learns that only other cops understand. This bond brings them closer. Soon they are vacationing together, bowling, eating, and, sometimes, sleeping together. Shared excitement and danger tightens the connection.

The pressures to conform are inexorable, the pleasures of membership exhilarating, and the pains of exclusion excruciating.

There are few more unifying experiences than sharing a moment of risk in the early morning hours and depending on your buddies to cover your back. It is something understood also by men and women in combat.

Gradually and through repeated reinforcements or sanctions, the young cop is shaped into an acceptable member of a very insular fraternity. The pressures to conform are inexorable, the pleasures of membership exhilarating, and the pains of exclusion excruciating.

Acculturation

The entire process of acculturation takes a few years of responding to calls, encountering the dangerous or unpredictable spikes that dot the often boring landscape, and shared moments that form the basis for bedrock attachments.

Ask any cop who his best friend is and if the answer is anything but "my partner" you are looking at a troubled worker. Cops' wives recite the complaint that their husbands care more for their partners than they do for their spouses.

The advent of women in the ranks has changed the inner reality in some ways. They are now, after a quarter century of entering in numbers, often a civilizing presence in a harsh, formerly all-male environment. A few have also given literal expression to the love cops feel for their partners, in acceptable forms. There is a bit of "friggin' in the riggin'," in the words of the late Admiral Elmo Zumwalt.

Such a thing as "the police character" exists uniquely because of the power of the institution to shape and condition its members. This is the process of inuring the psyche to gore and repulsiveness, overcoming the inhibitions normally applied to the use of violence, and drawing on cynicism as a way of assessing the human animal's potential to wreak havoc.

A suspicious nature leads to the discovery of the evil behind innocent appearances. It is a useful tool. Cops evolve into veterans by developing the mechanisms essential to their effective functioning, even as these approaches strike dissonant chords with the larger community.

Although cops are shaped into cynics, it is indisputable that, in general, a certain identifiable segment is attracted to police work and this might be described as the more macho segment of the blue-collar population.

The masculine police world is aggressively libidinous. What this means is that contacts with women—at traffic stops, for example—have to be monitored and controlled. It also means a higher-than-normal level of sensitivity is essential to combat sexual harassment or exploitation within the ranks. Like the military, the world of cops is too often given to the excesses of sexual predators—at all levels and ranks.

In the end, the result—the formation of the hardened cop—occurs from the hundreds of blows struck and caresses bestowed by an organization endlessly reinforcing the messages that insure its survival and which protect the secrets essential to that viability.

Cops also learn that moral courage is not prized.

A thumper declaims, "*The job* (surprisingly this is the universal appellation the cops give their profession, as if no other form of employment could be contemplated) sucks; the chief is a psycho; we're going to hell in a handbasket and morale has never been lower than at this precise minute." These are among the usually accepted internal verities. It would be unthinkable for any other cop in the room to contradict such assertions, even if a contrary view is deeply felt and possible to demonstrate.

The moral courage to stand up and disagree or to point out wrongdoing or to remonstrate when someone is committing a brutal or corrupt act has been systematically exorcised from the body. Nothing is rarer than dissidents publicly disagreeing with their colleagues about the codes of conduct, as is clearly evident from the cover-ups and studied silences accompanying serious acts of wrongdoing. Whistle blowers, reformers, and other troublemakers are "snitches and rat finks" and all ranks are to close against these menaces.

Not one of the scores of LAPD [Los Angeles Police Department] cops witnessing or participating in the assault on Rodney King, a black male, in March 1991, interceded to stop the brutality or volunteered to come forward to testify against colleagues who were clearly involved in an egregious criminal act.

Frank Serpico peddled his case against corruption within the ranks of the NYPD, first to the very authorities charged with attacking such problems. He was a plainclothes cop assigned to enforce vice, gambling, and liquor violations in 1971 and—remarkably and uniquely—appalled to discover corruption in the ranks. He was shocked to discover the studied indifference of NYPD executives who had carefully nurtured reputations as the very nemeses of rogue cops.

The moral courage to stand up and disagree or to point out wrongdoing or to remonstrate when someone is committing a brutal or corrupt act has been systematically exorcised from the body.

Serpico then took his case of gambling payoffs and other crimes to the NYPD's superiors at City Hall but, unwilling to rile the cops with another long, hot summer in the offing, with its threat of more riots in Harlem, got sloughed off again.

It was not until he went to the *New York Times'* ace police reporter,

David Burnham, and the story appeared on page one, that officialdom was reluctantly galvanized into real action.

The overwhelming majority of cops are dedicated, noble workers, but the unstated truth is that they are all complicit in the code of silence.

The mayor appointed the Knapp Commission. He named Patrick V. Murphy the one and only *reform* police commissioner in the department's recent history; he, incidentally lasted only thirty months. Murphy was given the peg on which to hang a series of sweeping changes that, by his exit in May 1973, had the NYPD at unprecedented levels of cleanliness in terms of systemic brutality and corruption. Individual, ad hoc acts would continue to bedevil the agency, as they do all organizations, but the worst connections had been shattered. The department thereafter lived off these dramatic changes as it drifted back into such behaviors. . . .

Rotten and other apples

So what is a citizen to make of all of this?

A scandal breaks and the chief trots out the favored litany, "The vast majority of our cops are honest, dedicated public servants. These guys [the accused] are just a few rotten apples in an otherwise healthy barrel." This hoary phrase has served police execs faithfully since Bobby Peel started the bobbies.

The truth, however, is otherwise.

The overwhelming majority of cops are dedicated, noble workers, but the unstated truth is that they are all complicit in the code of silence. This includes the determination to cover up for each other, at least for as long as the charges don't include organizational "betrayals," as we will see, and which others might call "whistle blowing."

As the rookie is conditioned he has to be offered a menu of choices. He can stay reasonably clean and uninvolved and continue to function or he can partake of the goodies. The great majority choose noninvolvement in the raunchier pursuits but get along by going along with the demand for silence and, sometimes, backing up the accused cop. In the latter case the preferred strategy is blissful ignorance: "I wasn't there," or "I didn't see it," or some variation thereof. To the degree possible, associates are supported but in no case are they to be contradicted.

And therein lies the problem. The Code of Silence demands full and total participation. It is the price of admission and by accepting it, as all do—even those destined to rise in the ranks or who are already there—they become tainted. Even the cops who stay totally out of the seamier aspects, who wouldn't even accept a free cup of coffee, must be a part of the code of silence or risk the scorn—and worse—of all the members.

Thus policing becomes a sort of permanent, floating conspiracy of insiders against the larger public without. The clean and the unclean can be described as the "grass eaters" and the "meat eaters" (the more ferocious and aggressive members).

One curious artifact of this culture is that court records abound with sworn assurances from countless cops and chiefs that they'd never heard of a code of silence and that it doesn't exist. No judge in America, however, is free of the knowledge of this unspoken code and a host of other brazen police mendacities.

The code and "testilying"

I received a call recently from a federal judge who interrupted a trial midway through its course when three cops testified, one after the other, that they'd never heard of the code and that it didn't exist.

A search warrant for drugs was being executed on an apartment when a black woman walked by on the sidewalk in front of the building. She was swept up and roughly rushed into the apartment, strip-searched, and after an hour reluctantly released. She, to everyone's surprise, sued. No one expected a "street person" to complain.

Now the cops, under oath, described the textbook perfection of the warrant's execution and justified the detention of the woman as reasonable and good police practice. When they added the palpable fiction that no such code of silence existed, the judge "just lost it." He stopped the proceedings and called to see if I'd testify in the case as a neutral expert witness. I accepted.

I met with the lawyers immediately.

The city attorney for the cops had been perfectly content to have a compliant jury, very likely mostly white, sop up the police fictions. He knew that white America loves and trusts its cops, whatever the police protestations to the contrary. Now he blanched visibly as I described the gravamen of my forthcoming testimony.

The next day the judge called to thank me and to tell me to stop my work on the case. The cops' lawyer had hied to the city rulers and spelled out what is, in another euphemism, artfully described as the city's "potential exposure." The city decided to settle lest they be depicted in the media as racists. I was sure the settlement would be a high figure. The judge told me the city was giving the woman a quarter of a million dollars and paying her legal fees, as well as mine. I received $1,233 for my efforts.

So much for the sanctity of the cops' sworn testimony.

The cops call this "testilying." Clearly they feel no shame in it.

Yes, it turns out to be true—the barrel does contain mostly healthy apples but these are content to live in uneasy symbiosis with the rotten.

4

Police Are Pressured to Be Corrupt

Julius Wachtel

Julius Wachtel, a lecturer in criminal justice at Cal State Fullerton, re-tired from the Bureau of Alcohol, Tobacco, and Firearms in 1998 after twenty-five years in law enforcement.

Despite intensive efforts to curb police corruption, corruption still continues. The very nature of police work—dealing with criminals day after day with little supervision—encourages corruption. Police are judged by their superiors and by the public on their ability to catch criminals and reduce crime. As long as they are measured by these goals, police will feel pressure to cut corners—such as planting evidence and ignoring a suspect's civil rights. Adopting more stringent standards of police training is an important step in reducing the forces that lead to misconduct, but it is not the only cure. The police culture and the environment that demands results must also be changed in order to achieve a long-term solution for police corruption.

New York City. Washington, D.C. New Orleans. Los Angeles. What do these four cities have in common? Police misconduct. Since inception of the first regularized force in the U.S., in New Amsterdam (later New York City), cycles of what criminologist Lawrence Sherman termed "scandal and reform" have plagued the police in urban America.

The usual suspects

On each occasion, civilian and police investigating commissions have conducted thorough probes. And after much chest-thumping and self-flagellation, each has pointed to the same list of "usual suspects": poor hiring practices, lax supervision, ineffective internal inspection mechanisms, the absence of executive leadership and so on.

The ultimatum presented to the Los Angeles Police Department . . . by Bill Lann Lee, acting assistant attorney general in the Justice Department's Civil Rights Division, follows in this tradition: "Serious deficiencies in LAPD [Los Angeles Police Department] policies and procedures for training, supervising and investigating and disciplining police officers foster and perpetuate officer misconduct." Other than Lee's insistence on external oversight, his dicta that more management is better management mirrors the conclusions of the LAPD's own exhaustive Board of Inquiry report, which is at present the *mea culpa* to beat.

Why are we still stuck on the same track? What has been the benefit of extending police training so that rookies endure academies lasting six months or more? What is the benefit of spending hundreds of millions to support the National Institute of Justice and millions more on police executive training at the FBI Academy and elsewhere? What is the benefit of the proliferation of college criminal justice curricula, where it is now possible to earn everything from an associate degree to a Ph.D.? And, yes, what is the benefit of raising police salaries from mere subsistence to a level that allows a majority of police to enjoy the perquisites of the middle class?

Real officers on a crusade have rationalized virtually anything that held the promise of securing the desired outcome, including brutality and planting evidence.

Adopting ever-more stringent standards seems sensible. Sometimes we need to rearrange the deck chairs. Yet how far should we go? Should we install a sergeant in the back seat of every patrol car? How about a lieutenant instead? Better yet, let's clone the chief and. . . .

As every parent knows, merely tightening the screws cannot, in the long haul, overcome the forces that impel misconduct. This is equally true for policing. Thirty years ago, political scientist James Q. Wilson's landmark study, "Varieties of Police Behavior," suggested that police work is shaped by the environment. Simply put, we get the style of law enforcement that the community—or at least its politicians and more influential members—expects.

So-called "aggressive" policing could not have taken place in New York City in the absence of a demand to stem street crime. Abuses at Rampart [a department in the Los Angeles Police Department, and the site of the city's worst corruption scandal] did not start with a conspiracy between rogue officers; they began with a problem of crime and violence that beset Pico-Union. Into this web of fear and disorder, we dispatched officers—members of the ineptly named CRASH unit—whose mission it was to reclaim the streets for the good folks.

Did we supply officers with special tools to help them accomplish their task? Of course not, since none exist. Yet our expectations remained high. Police officers gain satisfaction from success. Their work is also judged by superiors, who are more interested in numbers of arrests than in narrative expositions, the latter being difficult to pass up the chain of command and virtually impossible to use in budget fights at City Hall.

Officers who volunteer for specialized crime-fighting assignments want to do more than take reports. They want to make a difference. For some, the poisonous brew of inadequate tools and pressures to produce have predictable consequences. Their dilemma is characterized by criminologist Carl Klockars as the "Dirty Harry" problem: given a lack of means, how to achieve good ends? Harry adopted bad means. Real officers on a crusade have rationalized virtually anything that held the promise of securing the desired outcome, including brutality and planting evidence. As their moral decay progressed, many even justified clearly self-serving behaviors, such as stealing money and evidence.

Long-term solutions

What is to be done? By all means, apply whatever management remedies are available. But for a long-term solution, look to the environment of policing and particularly to the self-induced and agency-generated pressures that can spur vulnerable practitioners to cross the line.

For example:

• *Examine the mission.* If it cannot be done—and done well—with the resources at hand, reconsider the approach. Emphasize conventional tactics, particularly uniformed patrol, and lobby forcefully for lasting remedies such as economic, social and educational investment.

• *Set realistic objectives.* This reduces the pressure to breach ethical boundaries. Quantitative measures can corrode the ethics of officers and distort the nature of their work. Instead of just "numbers," employ qualitative measures of performance. It may be less convenient than checking boxes on a form, but there is no satisfactory alternative.

• *Don't exaggerate.* Chiefs and command staffs must ensure that they—and their fellow decision-makers in city government—have realistic expectations about what the police can accomplish.

Yes, critical self-study is a good thing. Yet failure to attend to the forces that drive police work only promises to deliver an even thicker set of *mea culpas* the next time around.

5

Police Corruption Is Fueled by the War on Drugs

Joseph D. McNamara

Joseph D. McNamara is a retired police officer who started his career as a beat patrolman in New York City. He was also chief of police for Kansas City, Missouri, and San Jose, California, before retiring after thirty-five years of serving in law enforcement. He is also a fellow of criminal justice at Harvard Law School and an outspoken critic of the War on Drugs.

The War on Drugs has a powerful corrupting influence on police forces across the country because police officers know that they can rob drug dealers with impunity. No dealers or buyers are going to report a police officer stealing from them because they know that they themselves will be arrested. The corruption of police officers begins gradually, with the officers finding rationalizations for stealing the drug money. Then the corruption is perpetuated by the police code of silence, an unwritten rule that prohibits police officers from informing on one another's misconduct. As long as the War on Drugs continues, honest and innocent young officers will be transformed into corrupt gangsters.

When I retired from police work in 1991, I did not retire my interest in law enforcement, or in the communities that police serve, or in the Drug War. These interests continue unabated, and I still hope that I will see the end of the Drug War in my lifetime. The Drug War is not only ruining society, it is corrupting police forces across the country, and it will continue to do so as long as our current policies are in place.

The Drug War and corruption

I have been gathering evidence of this fact in researching my forthcoming book, *Gangster Cops: The Hidden Cost of America's War on Drugs*. In my research I've been horrified to uncover a pattern of thousands of predatory crimes committed by police officers in the past 30 years that are all connected to the Drug War. In studying these crimes, I've discovered two things:

First, the nature of the Drug War encourages, almost demands, corruption.

Second, the corruption bred by the Drug War is happening across the country, from police officer to police chief or sheriff.

We've got 2 million people behind bars in America today, and it is because cops are doing a good job of catching people. With politicians urging them to make high numbers of drug arrests, state and local police managed to make 1.4 million drug arrests last year for possession, mostly for low amounts, and mostly in low-income minority neighborhoods. But when we look at the nature of the drug crimes, we have to wonder just how it is that police could make such an impressive number of arrests. The fact is, drug crimes are far different from violent crimes such as robbery, rapes, and murder. Drug crimes involve consensual transactions. Unlike violent crimes, there are no victims and witnesses. The fact is, no participants in a satisfactory drug transaction have any motivation to press charges against one another. So how do we arrest 1.4 million people who don't have any victims pressing charges or providing evidence to help make the arrests?

The nature of the Drug War encourages, almost demands, corruption.

Rarely does it happen that a cop pulls a guy over and says, "I'd like to look in your trunk," and the driver says, "Sure, officer, I've got a kilo of cocaine in there, but I don't want you to think that I don't cooperate with the local police." Equally unlikely is a scenario where an ounce of cocaine is sitting on the dashboard, or the suspect throws a baggie at the cop's feet, for the cop to conveniently find. Situations like these certainly don't happen 1.4 million times a year. So the only way to achieve these numbers is if the cops take shortcuts. And they do. They regularly ignore the 4th Amendment and search people illegally. The fact is that over the years a corruption of the basic integrity in the criminal justice system has occurred. Often, the police officer on the witness stand is not, in fact, telling the truth. And often it is an otherwise good cop who is lying—yet he still believes that he's a good cop. He believes that in drug cases he's morally justified to illegally search someone and perjure his testimony. This belief is so prevalent, that the New York Police Department (NYPD) jokingly refers to a cop's perjury as "testilying." In the Los Angeles Police Department (LAPD), they call it joining the Liars' Club.

Gangster cops

This corruption exists not just among a few individuals scattered across the country, but among corrupt gangs of cops. These gangs have surfaced in big cities and small towns as well as rural areas across America. We cannot end cop gangsterism by merely plucking a few bad apples from the barrel. We can only end it by ending the Drug War policies that breed it.

When I speak of gangsterism, I'm talking about serious, predatory crimes committed by sworn officers of the law. Predatory felonies are different from an earlier type of corruption, which I call the Serpico Model, which involved police officers accepting bribes from gangsters to look the other way. Now, thanks to the climate created by our drug laws, we have something more ominous—small gangs of cops who are the gangsters. They've committed murders, kidnapping, and armed robberies—sometimes for, and sometimes against, drug dealers. And I'm not talking about the occasional case, or one department that is well known for having a bad reputation. I'm talking about big and small departments; even uniformed police officers committing armed robberies in uniform. One such case involved a Bronx police officer who was charged in 11 murders which he committed for a drug gang, although he pled guilty to only eight.

How is it that officers sworn to arrest drug dealers end up working for the dealers? Or stealing from them and murdering them? For one thing, the cops know perfectly well that drug dealers can't pop into the local police station and say, "Hey, some cop just robbed me of a kilo of cocaine and $25,000," because the dealer's facing life in prison for that. So the cops essentially have complete immunity from prosecution.

A case in point occurred some 10 years ago, when a predatory gang of crooked cops formed in the Los Angeles Sheriff's department. Their activities only came to light when the department received a letter from a woman who said she was tired of living like a Mafia wife. Her husband was a narc, and he and his team were robbing drug dealers and bragging about the money. When the department finally decided to investigate, they found that the cops had been living beyond their means. Although they made between $30,000 and $35,000, they owned $500,000 homes and vacation homes. The department with help from the feds ran a sting and caught the squad supervisor stealing money. To lighten his sentence, the supervisor gathered evidence against his team members and other cops. In addition, a couple of other members of the gang also "ratted," as they say, on their colleagues.

Cops essentially have complete immunity from prosecution.

In contrast, in the case of Rafael Perez, a decorated, gung-ho LAPD officer convicted of stealing cocaine from the LAPD evidence room, there was no sting operation to uncover further corruption. Even though Perez was found guilty of stealing cocaine, no one thought to question his testimony in a trial two years earlier involving Perez and Javier Francisco Ovando. Perez had testified that Ovando had tried to kill him and his partner, and that they shot back in self-defense, wounding Ovando in the head. If the department had investigated, they would have found that Perez and his partner had lied about Ovando, and committed other violent crimes.

The truth only came to light when Perez was charged with *other* crimes, and decided to come clean in return for a lighter sentence. To achieve that goal, Perez confessed that he and his partner had handcuffed and shot Ovando in the head. They had then planted a sawed-off rifle on the 18-year-old boy and testified in court that he had tried to kill them. Miraculously, Ovando survived, although he is crippled for life. He was present when Perez perjured himself. Later, the judge castigated Ovando for endangering these vulnerable officers, then sentenced Ovando to 23 years in prison.

Corruption among our narcotics officers will go on no matter what.

Once the truth came out, it was easy to claim that Perez was a "bad apple." But an examination of his life showed the opposite. Growing up in Philadelphia, Perez hated drug dealers. He served in the Marine Corps for four years before becoming a police officer. He was such a gung-ho cop that he was put in a special street crimes unit, and then into drug enforcement.

Similarly, one of the sheriff's deputies who had been stealing from dealers had been named California Narcotics Association Officer of the Year. The rotten apple explanation doesn't explain the behavior of these officers.

Perez's victim is of course now out of prison, but the damage to him is done and it can't be undone. As the Ramparts scandal continues to be investigated, more allegations are being made. But still we have to wonder how many other, unknown victims like Ovando are out there, elsewhere in America, waiting to be discovered? As long as the Code of Silence holds, we'll never know.

There are over 600,000 sworn police officers in the United States, in 19,000 police operations, and almost all of them buy into the Code of Silence, which ensures that police officers do not inform on one another. This code existed before the Drug War, but since the Drug War it has been critical in shielding gangster cops from prosecution. The Code of Silence originated because police live in a world that is very different from that of the average citizen, and so police tend to be twice as cynical as the average citizen. They look at each other and say, "We are the only ones who know what this is all about. The citizens don't understand. They see the defendant the next day in the courtroom with his lawyer and he's calm and he presents himself as a reasonable citizen; they didn't see him trying to kill me last night." So police believe that because they are dealing with criminals they are justified in engaging in bad behavior. The people they're dealing with could kill them at any moment. So the rules for dealing with criminals slowly become different from the rules they have for dealing with an innocent, upstanding citizen.

Extra protection

Police unions also support the Code of Silence, by giving police a little more due process than the average citizen receives. In New York City, for instance, the very same officers who may dissuade suspects from calling their lawyer when they bring them in for questioning do not have to make a statement for 48 hours if they are suspected of wrongdoing. This policy exists in many other cities across the country. In addition, police routinely take the 5th Amendment, even when they're absolutely right, and they get what we call reverse Miranda. In fact, the ones who demand Miranda the most are police officers. In California, they also have what we call the police officers' Bill of Rights, in which an officer must be given an administrative Miranda warning and has a right to have an attorney present if any conversation is to take place that might result in the officer's being disciplined.

The philosophy of the unions and of the departments is typically this: because police put themselves in harm's way to protect us, they should get promoted for making good arrests and for solving cases—not for being diligent about protecting people's constitutional rights.

Nevertheless, now and then abuses occur that cannot be ignored. Yet even in these cases, it can be difficult to punish an officer—in part because of the protections offered by the unions, and in part because policing is very political, and politicians feel compelled to outdo each other in declaring war on crime and war on drugs. They all want the endorsements of the police unions, and all police serve under politicians, from mayors to city councils. As San Jose police chief, I found out firsthand how the politicians and the police union make it almost impossible to punish police officers.

With such systems in place to protect police, and as long as the Drug War continues, gangster cops will continue to be formed out of even the raw material of cops who joined the force as good and honest men.

The fact is, the amount of money involved in black market drug dealing offers cops an incredible temptation. The LA Sheriff's department officers stole millions of dollars. And when they were caught, they used the same words as the gang of cops who had been living like kings in the Bronx, off the proceeds of stolen drugs and cash: "Why," they asked, "should the enemy get to keep all the money?"

Corruption among our narcotics officers will go on no matter what. So long as cops are pressured to fulfill a drug arrest quota, they'll feel justified in making illegal searches and committing perjury concerning the circumstances of the arrest. They'll commit these felonies as long as they produce the kind of statistics that the brass wants. And many will follow the road of temptation, from theft right on down to murder.

It is true that it's only a small percentage of the total number of police officers that ever commit these crimes. But they do enormous damage—not only to their victims and the community, but to honest cops.

This is tragic. But what is more upsetting is the fact that it is an avoidable tragedy. In asking the police to fight the Drug War, we are asking them to do something that really can't be legally done in the first place. And now we're asking them to try to do it better. In the process, we've created a monster that is eating away at something far more important to the country than drug use, and that is the integrity of and belief in our criminal justice system.

6

Drug-Related Police Corruption Differs from Other Forms of Police Corruption

Richard M. Stana

Richard M. Stana is the director of justice issues at the U.S. General Accounting Office in Washington, D.C.

Drug-related corruption differs from other types of police corruption. Drug-related corruption includes officers stealing drugs or money from drug dealers, selling drugs, or lying under oath about illegal searches. Officers involved in this type of corruption are actively committing crimes, as opposed to other types of police corruption where the police are either protecting criminals or ignoring their behavior. Several factors are consistently associated with drug-related police corruption: the police culture, characterized by a code of silence; the maturity and education levels of the police officers; ineffective management that does little to promote integrity or supervise officers; opportunity to commit corruption; inadequate training; police brutality; and personal ties to an officer's neighborhood. The primary motive for drug-related police corruption is money, although other factors such as the police culture and ineffective supervision are also identified.

R ecent police corruption cases in several cities, including New York, Chicago, and Philadelphia, highlight the association of police corruption with illegal drug activities. You [Congressman Charles B. Rangel] asked us [General Accounting Office, Administration of Justice Issues] to study the impact of drug trafficking on the corruption of police in large cities that have a high incidence of drug trafficking and drug abuse. As agreed with your office, in conducting our preliminary work, we sought to identify commission reports and research studies on drug-related cor-

Excerpted from "Law Enforcement—Information on Drug-Related Police Corruption," by Richard M. Stana, report to U.S. Rep. Charles B. Rangel, May 28, 1998.

ruption in city police departments, as well as to identify relevant databases and other pertinent information.

We did not locate any central data sources that would allow us to reliably estimate the extent of police corruption or how much of corruption is drug-related. However, the reports and studies we reviewed, as well as our interviews with officials and academic experts, provided descriptive information on the (1) nature and extent of known drug-related police corruption in certain large cities; (2) factors associated with known drug-related police corruption; and (3) practices that have been recommended or implemented to prevent or detect drug-related police corruption. . . .

Officers involved in drug-related corruption were more likely to be actively involved in the commission of a variety of crimes.

To determine what information was available on drug-related police corruption, we (1) conducted a literature search and review to identify relevant commission reports, academic studies, symposium results, and other literature; . . . (2) interviewed academic experts on police corruption and members and/or staffs of two anti-police-corruption commissions— one in New York City and the other in Chicago; (3) interviewed officials with the Department of Justice (DOJ) and Federal Bureau of Investigation (FBI) in Washington, D.C., the U.S. Attorneys' Offices for the Eastern and Southern Districts of New York, and the Office of National Drug Control Policy (ONDCP); and (4) contacted international, national, and state law enforcement associations, including the International Association of Chiefs of Police (IACP). In addition, we met with officials from the New York City Police Department's (NYPD) Internal Affairs Bureau (IAB) and the current New York City Commission to Combat Police Corruption.

The Commission to Investigate Allegations of Police Corruption and the Anti-Corruption Procedures of the Police Department, commonly referred to as the Mollen Commission, was established in July 1992 by an executive order of New York City Mayor David N. Dinkins. The commission was given a threefold mandate: (1) to investigate the nature and extent of corruption in the New York City Police Department, (2) to evaluate the department's procedures for preventing and detecting corruption, and (3) to recommend changes and improvements in those procedures. The commission issued its report in July 1994 and was subsequently disbanded.

The Commission on Police Integrity, also referred to as the Chicago Commission, was appointed on February 7, 1997, by Chicago Mayor Richard M. Daley. The commission's charge was to examine the root causes of police corruption, to review how other urban police departments approach the issue, and to propose possible changes to Chicago Police Department policies and procedures. The commission issued its first report in November 1997 and was still active as of April 1998.

In response to a recommendation of the Mollen Commission, the New York City Commission to Combat Police Corruption was created on February 27, 1995, by an executive order of Mayor Rudolph W. Giuliani. The New York City Commission was established to monitor the performance of the NYPD's systems for combatting corruption. This commission is charged with, among other things, performing audits, studies, and analyses to assess the quality of these systems.

We did our work in Washington, D.C., and New York City, New York, from August 1997 through April 1998. The information we provide in this report is derived from our review of a limited number of existing reports and studies, as well as interviews with various officials and academic experts, not from any primary data collection or analysis undertaken by us. We did not attempt to verify the adequacy of the methodologies used to produce the various findings, nor did we attempt to assess the appropriateness of the conclusions. Accordingly, our presentation of the findings and conclusions of these reports and studies should not be construed as our endorsement of them. Moreover, we recognize that the policies and practices of the police departments discussed in the reports and studies may subsequently have changed. However, reviewing current policies and practices in particular departments was beyond the scope of this report. . . .

We provided copies of a draft of this report for a review of the facts, as presented, to various DOJ units and selected police organizations and academic experts. At an exit conference, we discussed the contents of the draft with DOJ officials, including the Criminal Division's Deputy Executive Officer and representatives of the Criminal Division's Public Integrity Section and Narcotic and Dangerous Drug Section, the Executive Office for U.S. Attorneys (EOUSA), and the Bureau of Justice Assistance. We also contacted the Chief of the FBI Criminal Investigative Division's Public Corruption Unit; the Commanding Officer, Office of Chief, NYPD's IAB; the Director of Research, IACP; Judge Milton Mollen (retired), former Chairman of the Mollen Commission; and Richard H. Ward, Professor of Criminal Justice, University of Illinois at Chicago and Executive Director for the Chicago Commission. The various officials and experts provided technical comments, which have been incorporated in this report where appropriate.

Results in brief

According to a number of commission reports, academic publications, and other literature we reviewed and the officials and academic experts we interviewed, drug-related police corruption differs in a variety of ways from other types of police corruption. In addition to protecting criminals or ignoring their activities, officers involved in drug-related corruption were more likely to be actively involved in the commission of a variety of crimes, including stealing drugs and/or money from drug dealers, selling drugs, and lying under oath about illegal searches. Although profit was found to be a motive common to traditional and drug-related police corruption, New York City's Mollen Commission identified power and vigilante justice as two additional motives for drug-related police corruption. The most commonly identified pattern of drug-related police corruption involved small groups of officers who protected and assisted each other in criminal activities, rather than the traditional patterns of non-drug-related police corruption that involved just a few isolated individuals or systemic corruption pervading an entire police department or precinct.

Regarding the extent of drug-related police corruption, data are not collected nationally. Federal agencies either do not maintain data specifically on drug-related police corruption or maintain data only on cases in which the respective agency is involved. Thus, it was not possible to estimate the overall extent of the problem. However, the academic experts and various officials we interviewed, as well as the commission reports, expressed the view that, by and large, most police officers are honest.

One . . . factor associated with drug-related corruption was a police culture that was characterized by a code of silence, unquestioned loyalty to other officers, and cynicism about the criminal justice system.

The FBI provided us with data on FBI-led drug-related corruption cases involving state and local law enforcement officers. However, since the total number of drug-related police corruption cases at all levels of government is unknown, the proportion constituted by FBI cases also is unknown. Data from local sources, if collected, pose several problems. For example, drug-related police corruption cases may not be readily identifiable from the offense charged or departments may view this information as proprietary or confidential and may not release it. Notwithstanding the lack of systematic data, the commissions and some academic experts described cases of drug-related police corruption in large cities such as Atlanta, Chicago, Cleveland, Detroit, Los Angeles, Miami, New Orleans, New York, and Philadelphia.

Factors associated with drug-related police corruption

Many of our sources consistently reported certain factors to be associated with drug-related police corruption, although these factors may also be associated with police corruption in general. Not every source identified every factor, and the sources differed to some degree on the emphasis to be placed on a factor. However, if all of the factors are considered together, they provide a consistent framework. Also, the factors discussed in this report may not encompass all factors associated with drug-related police corruption, since the identified factors are based on publicly reported incidents of drug-related police corruption.

One commonly identified factor associated with drug-related corruption was a police culture that was characterized by a code of silence, unquestioned loyalty to other officers, and cynicism about the criminal justice system. Such characteristics were found not only to promote police corruption, but to impede efforts to control and detect it. A second associated factor was the maturity (e.g., age) and education of police officers. Officers lacking in experience and some higher education were considered to be more susceptible to involvement in illicit drug-related activities.

Several of our sources also identified a variety of management-related factors associated with drug-related corruption. These factors included ineffective headquarters and field supervision, the failure of top police officials to promote integrity, and weaknesses in a police department's internal investigative structure and practices. In addition, on-the-job opportunities to commit illegal acts; inadequate training, particularly integrity training in the police academies and on the job; police brutality; and pressures arising from an officer's personal neighborhood ties were also believed by some sources to be associated with drug-related police corruption.

How to prevent or detect police corruption

Our sources also identified practices that they believed could prevent or detect drug-related police corruption. These practices, although often directed toward combatting police corruption in general, also were viewed as effective steps toward specifically addressing drug-related police corruption. Again, while every source did not conclude that every practice was effective or suitable for local conditions, considered together, the practices offer a starting point for prevention strategies.

Among the prevention practices that our sources identified were (1) making a commitment to integrity from the top to the bottom of the police department; (2) changing the police culture; (3) requiring command accountability (i.e., requiring a commitment to corruption control throughout the entire department, especially by field commanders); (4) raising the age and educational requirements and implementing or improving integrity training in the police academy for recruits; (5) implementing or improving integrity training and accountability measures for career officers; (6) establishing an independent monitor to oversee the police department and its internal affairs unit; and (7) community policing.

The detection practices our sources discussed included integrity testing, early warning systems to identify potential problem officers, and proactive investigations of individual officers or precincts with a high number of corruption complaints.

Lastly, we identified several federal initiatives that were directed toward assisting state and local governments in preventing and detecting police corruption.

Police corruption

Police corruption, according to the academic and other literature and anticorruption commission reports we reviewed, is not a new problem and dates back to the establishment of the first organized local police forces.

Community policing is an approach by which local police departments develop strategies to address the causes of and reduce the fear of crime through problem-solving tactics and community-police partnerships. Community policing programs stress three principles that make these programs different from traditional law enforcement programs: (1) prevention, (2) problem solving, and (3) partnerships.

Police integrity tests include "stings" designed to determine whether officers take advantage of opportunities to engage in corrupt practices that are presented to them by undercover operatives.

According to a report by the Knapp Commission, when the NYPD was established in 1844 as the first municipal police department in this country, it experienced immediate problems with extortion and other corrupt activities. Subsequently, the NYPD has experienced scandals and investigations approximately every 20 years. As in New York City, corruption has plagued police departments in many major cities at some point in their history, including Boston, Chicago, Detroit, Los Angeles, Miami, New Orleans, and Philadelphia.

Police corruption . . . is not a new problem and dates back to the establishment of the first organized local police forces.

While it has been a persistent problem for law enforcement, the nature of police corruption has varied over time. Historically, police corruption involved such low-level and passive activities as bribery schemes and nonenforcement of the law. Also, early police corruption was often depicted as the result of a few dishonest individuals—commonly referred to as "rotten apples"—in an otherwise honest department. However, during the police corruption scandals of the 1970s and 1980s, the corruption uncovered in several cities was found to be systemic, rather than attributable to individual behavior.

During the 1970s, New York City's Knapp Commission identified two general forms of police corruption, which it referred to as "grass-eaters" or "meat-eaters." According to the Knapp Commission's report:

> The overwhelming majority of those [police officers] who do take payoffs are "grass-eaters," who accept gratuities and solicit five- and ten- and twenty-dollar payments from contractors, tow-truck operators, gamblers, and the like, but do not aggressively pursue corruption payments. "Meat-eaters," probably only a small percentage of the force, spend a good deal of their working hours aggressively seeking out situations they can exploit for financial gain, including gambling, narcotics, and other serious offenses which can yield payments of thousands of dollars.

The Knapp Commission concluded that, while the meat-eaters receive the large payoffs and the newspaper coverage, the grass-eaters are the heart of the problem because their greater numbers make corruption respectable. . . .

Defining police corruption

Despite this history, disagreement still exists among criminal justice practitioners, researchers, and the public as to what type of behavior constitutes police corruption. Some definitions include behavior that ranges from brutality to questionable behavior such as verbal attacks on citizens. Two key elements of the various definitions of police corruption, as found in the academic literature we reviewed, are that the acts involve (1) the "misuse" of the officer's professional role—"authority" or "official position"—and (2) the receipt or expected receipt of material rewards or personal gain.

Enforcement of laws against all forms of vice (e.g., gambling, prostitution, and drugs) reportedly afford opportunities for police corruption. However, drug enforcement often exposes police officers to large amounts of cash and drugs held by individuals who are not likely to complain about illegal police behavior. Recent newspaper accounts, commission reports, academic studies, and other literature we reviewed suggest that today there are more opportunities than in the past for drug-related police corruption.

Although the FBI and DOJ have jurisdiction for investigating and prosecuting public corruption, police corruption is generally investigated internally by local police departments and/or prosecuted by local district attorneys. The FBI, DOJ, and other federal agencies are involved in only some local public corruption cases, including police corruption, and the extent of that involvement varies among cities across the country.

Information about drug-related police corruption is limited

A number of the commission reports, academic publications, and other literature we reviewed and the officials and academic experts we interviewed described differences between the nature of drug-related police corruption and the nature of other types of police corruption; however, opportunities for financial gain were a key factor in both forms of corruption. Unlike other types of corruption, officers involved in drug-related corruption were found to be actively committing crimes, not just passively ignoring them or protecting criminals. These crimes ranged from stealing drugs and money from drug dealers to lying under oath about illegal searches. Usually these activities were carried out by small groups of officers, rather than by lone individuals. Moreover, drug-related police corruption was not found to be a systemic problem that infected entire departments or precincts. Although cases of drug-related police corruption have been identified in a number of large cities, we found that only limited data on the extent of the problem were available. . . .

Different types of police corruption

Several of our sources described differences between the types of illegal activities generally associated with drug-related police corruption and those associated with other types of police corruption. Traditional police corruption usually involved a mutually beneficial arrangement between criminals and police officers (e.g., the former offered the latter bribes in exchange for immunity from arrest). In contrast, several studies and investigations of drug-related police corruption found on-duty officers engaged in serious criminal activities, such as (1) conducting unconstitutional searches and seizures; (2) stealing money and/or drugs from drug dealers; (3) selling stolen drugs; (4) protecting drug operations; (5) providing false testimony; and (6) submitting false crime reports. According to NYPD officials, some police officers also engaged in drug-related crimes while off duty.

The Mollen Commission reported in 1994 that the most prevalent form of police corruption in New York City was police committing crimes, especially in connection with the illegal drug trade, whereas the

Knapp Commission reported about 20 years earlier that the prevalent form of corruption was police taking money to overlook illegal activities, such as bookmaking. In summary, the Mollen Commission, in contrast to the Knapp Commission, found that the meat-eaters, as opposed to the grass-eaters, had become the rule among corrupt police officers, rather than the exception.

Drug enforcement often exposes police officers to large amounts of cash and drugs held by individuals who are not likely to complain about illegal police behavior.

The types of reported drug-related corruption engaged in by police officers, as well as the types of police corruption tolerated, differed among cities and even differed among precincts within the same city. Several academic experts, as well as officials in New York City, indicated that the levels of acceptance for different types of offenses committed in connection with drug enforcement activities varied, and that the perceived line between corrupt and acceptable police behavior was not fixed. For example, some of these sources suggested that an officer might view stealing money from a drug dealer as acceptable behavior, while the officer would draw the line at stealing and selling drugs. Over time, behavior, such as dealing in illegal drugs, which was previously viewed as unacceptable by even corrupt officers might become acceptable or at least tolerated. However, our sources also indicated that formerly acceptable behavior, such as lying under oath, might become unacceptable. In addition, certain sources suggested that in one department, officers might be more likely to report drug-related corruption but not acts of brutality; while in another department, the reverse might be the norm.

Motives

As in the case of other types of police corruption, a primary reported motive for drug-related police corruption was financial gain, but profit was not the only motive identified. The Mollen Commission identified three motivating factors for corruption: (1) profit, (2) power, and (3) perceived "street" law enforcement ends. The commission further explained that while corrupt police officers usually raided drug locations for profit, they sometimes carried out raids because they (1) wanted to show that they were in control of the precinct's "crime-ridden streets," (2) wanted to feel the "power" and "thrill" of their badges and uniforms, or (3) believed that vigilante justice was the way to punish those who might otherwise go unpunished. Similarly, some of the officials we interviewed suggested such motives as job cynicism due to the perception that the revolving door of justice lets criminals go free, or officers' dissatisfaction with how they were viewed and treated by the people in the community.

Our sources also identified differences between the pattern of drug-related police corruption and patterns of other types of police corruption. The commissions and academic experts reported that drug-related police corruption typically involved small groups of officers. For example, the Mollen Commission described these groups, such as those found in New York City's 73rd precinct case, as "crews" akin to street gangs. Similarly, the Chicago Commission reported that the officers they surveyed characterized corruption as isolated in small groups. In other cities, identified drug-related police corruption cases usually involved from 9 to 30 officers often working together, not individuals or entire departments. Drug-related police corruption usually did not involve such non-drug-related patterns as (1) just a few isolated individuals within a department who engaged in illegal acts or (2) low-level corruption pervading entire departments or precincts.

The commission reports, as well as several federal and New York City officials and academic experts we interviewed, generally described drug-related police corruption as being organized differently from the corruption of earlier eras; however, these sources varied in their characterization of the new organizational forms. For example, in describing New York City's 30th precinct case, a DOJ official said that, although numerous officers were involved, it was not one large enterprise. Rather, officers moved in and out of groups, depending on how opportunities presented themselves. The Mollen Commission compared the "standardized and hierarchical—almost bureaucratic" organizational forms of traditional corruption with the street-gang-like structure of the drug-related crews, which were "small, loyal, flexible, fast moving and often hard hitting." The commission also noted that, in some cases, there were explicit agreements or pacts between officers to help ensure that officers observing criminal behavior would not report this behavior.

The Mollen Commission reported that in New York City's 73rd precinct between 1988 and 1992, a tightly knit group of 8 to 10 officers who worked together on steady tours of duty routinely conducted unlawful raids on drug locations while on duty.

The information sources used in this report generally concurred in their description of the nature of drug-related police corruption. However, since these sources' observations were based on publicly identified cases of such corruption, which may not be representative of all drug-related police corruption cases, these observations may not completely portray the nature of the problem.

Extent of drug-related police corruption is unknown

We did not locate any centralized, systematically gathered, nationwide source of data that could be used to estimate the extent of the problem nationally. Some data on drug-related police corruption were available from federal agencies, such as the FBI, and local agencies. These data usually included only information about cases in which the reporting organization had been involved or were of limited use because of inconsistencies or anomalies in the data-gathering and tabulating methodologies. However, our sources provided accounts of some drug-related police corruption cases in several large cities. . . .

During our review, we were unable to identify nationwide data sources for quantifiable information on the extent of drug-related police corruption. In this regard, we contacted appropriate DOJ agencies, including the

National Institute of Justice (NIJ), the Bureau of Justice Statistics, the Criminal Division's Public Integrity Section and Narcotic and Dangerous Drug Section, the FBI's Public Corruption Unit, and the Federal Bureau of Prisons (BOP); national and state police organizations; and academic experts in the field of police research. However, various academic experts and officials we interviewed and the commission reports reviewed expressed the view that, by and large, most police officers are honest.

During the course of its investigation in 1993, the Mollen Commission uncovered allegations of corruption against several officers in New York City's 30th precinct (Manhattan). The commission brought this information to the attention of city and federal officials. The U.S. Attorney for the Southern District of New York investigated the allegations with the commission; NYPD's IAB; and, subsequently, the local district attorney's office. Ultimately, 30 officers were convicted of primarily drug-related offenses. An additional officer was acquitted, but the officer was later found guilty of administrative charges and was fired by the NYPD. . . .

Some cases of drug-related police corruption

Our sources did identify examples of publicly disclosed cases of drug-related police corruption in several cities during the past decade. The Mollen Commission investigated and uncovered drug-related police corruption in New York City. The Chicago Commission described identified cases of drug-related police corruption in Chicago, New York City, Philadelphia, Miami, New Orleans, Los Angeles, and Detroit. In addition, we identified accounts of drug-related police corruption in Atlanta and Cleveland. . . .

However, since the publicized cases only provided information about those officers convicted of identified drug-related corruption offenses in cities where the problem had been reported, these individuals and cities may not be representative of officers who commit such offenses or of the locations where such crimes are committed. From the case information available, no conclusions can be drawn about (1) which types of officers are involved in drug-related corruption; (2) the extent of drug-related police corruption within cities where it has been identified; or (3) the incidence of drug-related police corruption in cities across the country.

Factors associated with drug-related police corruption

The commission reports, much of the academic and other literature we reviewed, and officials and academic experts we interviewed, identified a variety of factors as being associated with drug-related as well as other types of police corruption. These factors included (1) opportunities to commit illegal acts or crimes on the job—for example, the availability of large sums of money; (2) the maturity-level (age) and education-level of the officer; (3) inadequate training, particularly integrity training, in the police academies and on the job; (4) a police culture that supported or ignored corruption; (5) ineffective headquarters and field supervision; (6) management's failure to enforce a code of integrity; (7) weaknesses in a police department's internal investigative structure and practices; (8) involvement in police brutality; and (9) pressures arising from an officer's personal neighborhood ties.

Our sources did not rank the factors according to their impact on drug-related police corruption; therefore, we had no basis on which to assess their relative importance. Moreover, since these factors were only associated with identified drug-related police corruption cases that have been publicly disclosed, they may not be all inclusive or necessarily representative of the universe of drug-related police corruption cases. Also, to our knowledge, no systematic studies of the causal link of these factors to drug-related police corruption have been undertaken.

Opportunity

Our sources described police recruits, generally, as individuals who had become police officers for the right reasons. They also said that once on the job, however, officers working in precincts with a high level of drug activity may be confronted with opportunities to commit illegal acts or crimes, such as taking large sums of money from drug dealers, who are generally reluctant to complain about thefts by police officers. Without support and experience, these temptations are hard for some officers to resist. Moreover, federal officials, academic experts, and the commission reports described how some police officers who engaged in illicit drug-related activities were able, through a "de-sensitizing" or rationalization process, to justify their behavior on the basis of, for example, the notion that they were only harming or disrupting illegal drug dealers.

Officers involved in drug-related corruption were found to be actively committing crimes, not just passively ignoring them or protecting criminals.

Academic sources and DOJ Criminal Division Public Integrity Section officials suggested that police officers working in certain situations, such as in undercover operations, could be more vulnerable to involvement in illegal drug-related activities. For example, the nature of undercover work generally places an officer in a criminal environment conducive to corruption. In addition, these federal officials opined that corruption was more likely to result from day-to-day contacts between police officers and informants. Academic and other sources also suggested that special drug investigation units with low levels of supervision were also considered to be high-risk environments for drug-related corruption.

Maturity and education level

The commission reports we reviewed and various officials and academic experts we interviewed indicated that certain recruitment policies, such as lower age and education requirements, might be related to incidents of police corruption. An official in the U.S. Attorney's Office of the Southern District of New York and academic experts indicated that in New York City and Chicago, for example, most of the officers involved in recent drug-related corruption cases would not have been hired under previous higher age and education criteria.

Moreover, rapid recruitment initiatives to meet major, time-critical hiring demands appeared to be associated with episodes of drug-related police corruption in some cities. For example, police departments in Miami and Washington, D.C., went through major hiring initiatives during the 1980s, and these departments subsequently experienced corruption problems. Academic sources and some federal officials suggested that, for various reasons, including inadequate screening (e.g., inadequate or incomplete background checks), such rapid recruitment initiatives might have permitted the hiring of recruits who might not otherwise have been hired.

Inadequate police academy and on-the-job training

Inadequate training, particularly integrity training, in the police academies and especially on the job, was identified as another factor associated with drug-related corruption.

According to a member of the Mollen Commission we interviewed, before the establishment of the commission, and the implementation of its recommendations, the NYPD's integrity training consisted of the message "don't get caught." Moreover, the Mollen Commission found that the NYPD police academy's integrity training at that time was based on the types of corruption uncovered by the Knapp Commission, such as gambling and vice rackets. The Mollen Commission concluded that this training not only had little relevance to the temptations confronted by police officers about 20 years later, but the training sent a message of departmental disinterest in integrity matters. Asserting that the real test of the effectiveness of the Chicago Police Department's training strategies comes when new police officers are assigned to districts and begin to face the challenges inherent in their work, the Chicago Commission found that the department could do a better job in this crucial area.

NYPD officials told us that the integrity training program subsequently had been changed, and they provided us with a copy of the student training guide.

Police culture

The relationship between police culture and police corruption, including drug-related police corruption, was a recurring theme articulated by our various sources. They generally concurred that although police culture may be positive (i.e., supportive of integrity), a negative culture (i.e., one that supported or generally ignored corruption) was a key factor associated with drug-related police corruption. Among the attitudes and values identified as characteristics of a police culture that supported corruption were the following: (1) a code of silence with grave consequences for those violating it; (2) loyalty to other officers above all else; (3) police cynicism or disillusionment about their jobs, the criminal justice system, and public support for those who performed properly; and (4) indoctrination on the job as to what is acceptable behavior—for example, ignoring corruption. The Mollen Commission concluded that such aspects of a police culture primarily facilitated corruption by (1) setting the standard that nothing was more important than the loyalty of officers to each other (e.g., not stopping even the most serious forms of corruption) and (2) thwarting efforts to control corruption, thereby leading officers to cover up for other officers' crimes.

The literature we reviewed and some academic experts suggested that the relationship between culture and corruption is complex. For example, one expert asserted that police behavior was affected by three levels of culture: (1) the culture of the police profession in general, (2) the culture of a particular police department, and (3) the culture of the city. He also suggested that the code of silence may be a characteristic that is common to the culture of police departments in general, while attitudes toward brutality or stealing illegal drugs may be more a part of a particular police department's culture. The literature indicates that tolerance of corruption varies among cities and even within a city, over time. In addition, the previous discussion on the lack of integrity training suggests an acculturational process, whereby new officers learn the rationalizations and accepted behaviors from more experienced officers.

Ineffective supervision

At the systemic level, the commission reports identified poor or inadequate supervision in police departments from the top down—at headquarters and in the field—as a factor associated with corruption. For example, the Mollen Commission found a widespread breakdown in field supervision in the NYPD. The commission asserted that this breakdown fueled and protected the police corruption they observed, and it primarily blamed NYPD's management for the poor state of police supervision. The Chicago Commission found the Chicago Police Department lacking in supervisory accountability and emphasized the importance of the supervisory role of sergeant to an effective police organization.

Management's failure to enforce a code of integrity

Various sources acknowledged the critical role of department management in promoting ethics and integrity and the serious consequences of management's failure to provide such leadership. Although major police departments historically have distributed rules and guidelines proscribing unethical and potentially corruptive conduct, an article from a recent symposium sponsored by the FBI and Major City Chiefs Administrators concluded that these guidelines may be confusing or misleading, and consequently can contribute to corruption. Moreover, in some departments, operational goals conflict with written policies. For example, a police department may have rules, which are consistently enforced through disciplinary actions, against accepting gratuities from the business community with corresponding sanctions, but the chief and other high-ranking commanders may be the guests of these same business representatives at their country clubs. Also, police organizations have generally claimed the privilege of self-regulation. The Mollen Commission concluded that the failure of NYPD's corruption controls reflected the inevitable consequence of allowing the police to "police themselves."

Our sources identified problems in a police department's internal investigative structure and practices as another aspect of inadequate management associated with drug-related police corruption. Control was negatively affected by such factors as the lack of respect for internal affairs units; flaws in investigative techniques; the lack of resources; inadequately skilled internal affairs staff; the lack of autonomy of the internal affairs bureau; and the minimizing or concealing of police corruption incidents (e.g., by putting allegations of police corruption in a special file rather than initiating an investigation). By 1992, according to the Mollen Commission, NYPD's corruption control system had collapsed, but no one in the department had the incentive to fix what was broken. Also, the Chicago Commission reported hearing evidence of substantial delays in addressing the corruption in one district. At the same time, however, the commission asserted that the Chicago Police Department's leadership, particularly its Internal Affairs Division, should be given some credit for taking a proactive role in exposing recent police corruption scandals. . . .

Over time, behavior, such as dealing in illegal drugs, which was previously viewed as unacceptable by even corrupt officers might become acceptable or at least tolerated.

Our literature review and expert interviews indicated that cities varied in the structures, procedures, and practices employed to identify and investigate corruption. For example, New York used field associates—line officers recruited to report covertly to the internal affairs unit on any misconduct or illicit activities that they observed while at work—but other cities did not.

Police brutality

Among other factors that the commission reports and several academic experts we interviewed found could be associated with drug-related police corruption was police brutality. In Chicago, for example, one researcher found that, while not all officers involved in police brutality were also engaged in drug-related police corruption, a number of police officers involved in drug-related corruption also had histories of the use of excessive force. The Mollen Commission reported a similar finding. DOJ public integrity officials suggested that, if there is a violation of the civil rights of a drug dealer, little support for the dealer would come from other police officers; rather, the code of silence would likely be invoked, creating an environment supportive of corruption.

Pressures from an officer's personal neighborhood ties

Still another factor associated with drug-related police corruption and identified during our review was pressure arising from an officer's personal neighborhood ties. That is, some sources indicated that neighborhood ties to friends, family members, or even associates, for example in gang-plagued areas, might make it difficult for officers raised in those communities to avoid situations that promote corrupt behavior. Alternatively, however, some sources suggested that neighborhood ties might deter corruption because officers would have a stake in the community.

How to prevent and detect drug-related police corruption

The commission reports and many of the academic and other publications we reviewed and the officials and academic experts we interviewed identified and/or recommended various practices to prevent and detect drug-related police corruption. We did not evaluate and do not necessarily endorse these practices. Although these practices generally are said to address the previously discussed factors that are associated with drug-related police corruption, the practices may also combat other types of corruption.

The prevention practices that were identified included (1) making a commitment to integrity from the top to the bottom of the department, (2) changing the police culture, (3) requiring command accountability, (4) raising the age and educational requirements and implementing or improving integrity training in the police academy for recruits, (5) implementing or improving integrity training and accountability measures for career officers, (6) establishing an independent monitor to oversee the police department and its internal affairs unit, and (7) community policing.

Among the detection practices recommended and/or implemented were integrity testing, early warning systems to detect potential problem officers, and proactive investigations of individual officers or precincts with a high number of corruption-related complaints. Several factors, such as available resources or the culture of the department, affected the appropriateness or implementation of these practices in particular cities. While some departments were already implementing some of the recommended prevention and/or detection practices, a recommendation usually was based on the perceived merits of the practice, which were grounded in policing experience, rather than a formal evaluation of that practice.

7

Police Corruption Is Rampant

Jack Nelson

Jack Nelson is a reporter for the Los Angeles Times.

The fact that the number of police officers sent to federal prisons on charges of corruption has multiplied five times in four years indicates that police corruption is rampant throughout the United States. Police corruption is not a problem only in big cities; it has also spread to small towns and rural areas as well. Many jurisdictions are attempting to fight corruption by firing officers who lie to cover up criminal acts by their colleagues. Some criminal justice experts maintain that corruption within the ranks will never be completely eliminated because the temptations—in the form of seized drugs and drug money—are just too great to resist.

L aw enforcement corruption, sparked mostly by illegal drugs, has become so rampant that the number of federal, state and local officials in federal prisons has multiplied five times in four years, from 107 in 1994 to 548 in 1998, according to a . . . study.

The official corruption, which has raged for years in the nation's big cities, is also spreading to the hinterlands. "It's a big problem across the country, in big towns and small towns, and it's not getting any better," says Chicago Police Superintendent Mike Hoke.

Hoke was head of the force's narcotics unit until three years ago, when officials, suspecting that some officers were deeply involved in the drug rackets, put him in charge of internal affairs to begin an investigation that is still under way.

"So far, we've sent 15 police to the penitentiary," Hoke said. "And we're not done yet."

Los Angeles, New York, Cleveland, Philadelphia, Washington, New Orleans and Savannah, Georgia, are among the other cities that have experienced major law enforcement scandals involving illegal drugs in recent years. And many smaller communities, especially in the South and Southwest, have been hit by drug-related corruption in police or sheriff's departments.

Police officials from more than 50 major cities [met] in Sun Valley, Idaho . . . to review the new report, "Misconduct to Corruption," compiled by officials from 15 cities with assistance from the FBI.

The authors of the report sent questionnaires to 52 cities. Of the 37 that responded, all acknowledged continuing problems with general corruption and misconduct in 1997.

Altogether, they reported 187 felony arrests of officers and 265 misdemeanor arrests. Eighty-five officers were charged with illicit use of drugs, 118 with theft, 148 with domestic violence and nine with driving under the influence of alcohol.

The report cited several cases of officers robbing drug dealers. In Indianapolis, one of two officers charged with murdering a drug dealer during a robbery admitted that they had been robbing drug dealers for four years.

A big-city police chief, the report concluded, "can expect, on average, to have 10 officers charged per year with abuse of police authority, five arrested for a felony, seven for a misdemeanor, three for theft and four for domestic violence. By any estimation, these numbers are unacceptable."

Numbers tell only so much

"You can't just look at the numbers" in measuring the effect on the community of "a police officer abusing citizens through corruption," said Neil J. Gallagher, deputy assistant director of the FBI's criminal investigative division. "Corruption erodes public confidence in government."

Gallagher, as special agent in charge of the New Orleans FBI office several years ago, directed an investigation that led to convictions of 11 officers and a sweeping overhaul of the city's police department. Underlying causes of corruption there, he said, ranged from "severely underpaying officers to lack of training, poor selection of officers and very little command and control."

Some veteran police executives said that, despite recurring reports of corruption, they have the impression that the problem of police corrupted by drug money has subsided somewhat in recent years.

In this camp is Robert S. Warshaw, associate director of the National Drug Control Policy Office at the White House and former Rochester, New York, police chief. Warshaw said that law enforcement agencies have become much more aware of the problem and "there's a high level of accountability internally."

Many other experts see little or no abatement of police corruption. "It's going on all over the country," said former San Jose Police Chief Joseph McNamara, "and corruption ranges from chiefs and sheriffs on down to officers. Every week we read of another police scandal related to the drug war—corruption, brutality and even armed robbery by cops in uniform."

McNamara, now a research fellow at the Hoover Institution in Palo Alto, has concluded that preventing drug trafficking is "an impossible job."

"The sheer hopelessness of the task has led many officers to rationalize their own corruption," McNamara said. "They say: 'Why should the enemy get to keep all the profits?' Guys with modest salaries are suddenly looking at $10,000 or more, and they go for it."

Even veteran officers can succumb. One is Rene De La Cova, a federal

Drug Enforcement Administration supervisor in Fort Lauderdale, Florida, whose photograph ran in newspapers from coast to coast in 1989 when he took custody of Panamanian strongman Manuel A. Noriega from the U.S. military forces who had captured him. Five years later, De La Cova pleaded guilty to stealing $760,000 in laundered drug money and was sentenced to two years in prison.

Protecting others seen as a virtue

Police often work in a culture in which protecting their colleagues is a virtue. Ed Samarra, police chief in the Washington suburb of Alexandria, Virginia, learned that during his five years in the internal affairs section of Washington's police department.

"I never encountered an officer willing to talk about the conduct of another officer, even if he was videotaped committing a crime," Samarra said. "Some went to prison even though they could have remained free if they had agreed to cooperate."

More than 100 Washington officers were arrested during Samarra's five years in internal security. In every instance, he complained, the police union "said our responsibility is to defend our people regardless of whether they are guilty."

In Alexandria, by contrast, the police department has a reputation for zero tolerance of misconduct. The police union tells new officers to report misconduct by their colleagues. Those who lie, it warns, will be fired.

In Los Angeles County, Sheriff Sherman Block credited his own task force with directing an investigation from 1988 to 1994 that led to the conviction of 26 former narcotics deputies—about 13% of those assigned to narcotics enforcement—for skimming drug money they had seized.

Not all county officials agreed with Block that his aggressive internal investigation had been so successful that the scandal actually "somewhat enhanced" the sheriff's department's reputation. He was widely praised, however, for rooting out corruption and condemning the deputies for violating their oaths and dishonoring their badges.

Law enforcement corruption . . . has become so rampant that the number of federal, state, and local officials in federal prisons has multiplied five times in four years.

The Los Angeles Police Department, while sharply criticized for use of excessive force, has been remarkably free of corruption linked to money or drugs.

The independent commission that examined the department in the wake of the Rodney G. King beating noted in its 1991 report that the department had done "an outstanding job, by all accounts, of creating a culture in which officers generally do not steal, take bribes, or use drugs. The LAPD must apply the same management tools that have been successful in attacking those problems to the problem of excessive force."

New Orleans, which had one of the nation's most corrupt police departments in the early 1990s, is widely recognized today for its reforms—a sharp increase in hiring standards, pay increases of up to 25% and a reorganization and restaffing of the internal affairs unit.

New Orleans officials, working with the FBI, uprooted the bad cops and tightened controls that not only curbed corruption and drug dealing but also helped reduce homicide and other crime rates.

Sting operation becomes violent

In the FBI's New Orleans sting operation, undercover agents acted as drug couriers who were protected by police officers. The situation became so violent that at one point FBI agents overheard a policeman using his bugged patrol-car phone to order another policeman to kill a woman who had filed a brutality complaint against him. Ten minutes later, before the agents could act, the woman was shot to death.

An FBI memo on the killing noted that the undercover operation was terminated earlier than scheduled "because of the extreme violence exhibited by the officers, which included threats to kill the undercover FBI agents acting as couriers and also to steal the cocaine being shipped."

Eleven officers and a civilian police employee were convicted of corruption and about 200 police officers were fired.

In another major FBI sting operation [in 1998], 59 people in metropolitan Cleveland, including 51 law enforcement and corrections officers, were arrested on charges of protecting the transfer or sale of large amounts of cocaine.

Drug Enforcement Agency (DEA) Administrator Thomas A. Constantine, a former New York state police superintendent, said that many police departments have adopted policies similar to Alexandria's zero tolerance for misconduct. These departments, he said, have beefed up their internal security units and are recruiting better quality officers by providing better salaries and conducting thorough background checks.

But many police departments have failed to take these steps. Raymond Kelly, the U.S. Treasury Department's undersecretary for enforcement and a former New York City police commissioner, contended that many departments conduct inadequate background checks and some are using internal affairs units as "dumping grounds" for problem officers.

Kelly said that police forces should be careful to check the lifestyles of their drug investigators. "I've never seen an officer get involved in corruption to put food on the table," he said. "It's always for something like cars or drugs or girlfriends."

As New York's deputy police commissioner in 1992, Kelly headed an investigation of the department's internal affairs unit during a drug-linked corruption inquiry.

Kelly, seeking to become more directly involved in law enforcement and the war on drugs, has stepped down as the No. 2 Treasury Department official to become commissioner of the Customs Service. In that role . . . his first challenge will be to take a hard look at Customs' internal affairs unit.

8

Police Routinely Lie in Court to Convict the Guilty

Scott Turow

Scott Turow is a lawyer and the author of several novels.

Police officers frequently lie under oath. They either commit perjury to conceal their own crimes or else they testify about events they can no longer remember, which also constitutes perjury. Most police officers do not frame innocent people, but they do believe that it is acceptable to perjure themselves if they can help convict a suspect whom they believe is guilty. Moreover, in the officers' minds, the suspect need not have committed the crime in question; if the police believe the suspect is guilty of another crime equally deserving of a prison or jail sentence, the officers will willingly perjure themselves. Courts and lawyers must stand up and insist that police officers stop perjuring themselves on the stand.

The Los Angeles County district attorney's office said . . . that the city's metastasizing police scandal was likely to result in the overturning of hundreds of criminal convictions. Apparently a number of officers in the city's Rampart District planted evidence and perjured themselves to help get convictions; a few even became criminals themselves, dealing drugs and shooting competing dealers.

First Rodney King, then O.J. Simpson, now this. You don't need a degree in criminal science to know that something is wrong in Los Angeles.

Police often lie in court

Yet those of us in other places should not be too smug. Defense lawyers and even some prosecutors in most big cities will say that police officers frequently lie under oath. What happened in L.A. is extreme—very rarely do officers commit perjury to cover up their own criminal acts. But law enforcement officers are sometimes moved to lie, feeling they've been driven to do so by the complex requirements of the criminal justice system.

Years ago, the first case I tried as a federal prosecutor nearly unraveled because of testimony a Secret Service agent gave the grand jury. Parroting the case reports, he described watching his colleagues arrest the defendants for selling a stolen Treasury check. The problem? Later, preparing for trial, I learned that the agent hadn't been working on the day in question. When I brought that to light, the agent acknowledged his error but insisted that he had sincerely believed that he had been present at the arrest.

The judge accepted that and didn't throw out the indictment. But the agent's testimony underlines a fundamental problem for all law officers.

The police are expected to testify about events that have taken place months and even years earlier; they may have handled hundreds of other matters in the interim. Because case reports are inadmissible to support their testimony, the officers are expected to offer a crystalline recollection of matters that in all likelihood they can barely recall. It should be apparent to everyone involved—prosecutors, the judge, the jury—that this is, technically speaking, perjury. But nobody seems to regard an officer's lying in service to the truth as a grave social ill.

The problem is that because cops are professional witnesses, the system makes it easy for the few bad ones to develop considerable aplomb as they disserve the truth for their own ends. Tamar Toister, a public defender who represented a gang member who was shot and framed by Rampart District police in L.A., called the officers "the slickest, most polished witnesses" she had ever encountered.

Her remark reminded me of several officers I called before a federal grand jury long ago in a beating investigation. One by one, they calmly denied events that several medical experts said were firmly established by the physical evidence. I was infuriated at first, but I eventually developed a sort of aesthetic appreciation of their performances. Calm to the point of appearing limp, soft-spoken and unflappable, the cops convinced the grand jurors of their innocence, against all logic.

Most cases of police perjury are not related to corruption or self-protection. Police officers usually just want to convict the guilty. A friend of mine who has retired from the force refers to this as "tightening up a case," and it has its own compelling logic. A cop who has patrolled an area for a while has seen and heard enough to recognize the local bad actor. Why on earth wait to catch him in the act? Hassle him, let him know you're watching, stop him on sight and frisk him, and when you inevitably find dope or a gun in his clothing, testify that you saw a telltale bulge or a glassine envelope peeking from his pocket.

Cops who "tighten up" assume that they know the difference between lying to get the guilty and framing the innocent (and in my experience, most of them do). But the line between the two often wears perilously thin.

I once represented one of two men who had been convicted of a celebrated murder they didn't commit. Eventually, my client and the other man were freed, and four police officers and three prosecutors were indicted on charges of concocting the case. (The officers and prosecutors were later acquitted.) When those indictments came down, another police officer from the area surprised me with his selective indignation over what the officers were alleged to have done: Framing someone like my client for burglary, he said, would be one thing, since the man was reputed to be a thief; framing him for murder, however, would be going too far.

The Los Angeles scandal lies only a couple of stops further down the slippery slope. Consider what a former police official in Los Angeles . . . said about those framed by Rampart officers: "We're talking about people who belonged in prison, just not for those reasons." He added, "The police may have stepped over the line, but they had to be tough with these people—let's be honest."

Refusing to turn a blind eye

It is no platitude to say that most cops are honest, and there are many departments that refuse to turn a blind eye to what some believe the system compels. The F.B.I. in most places and the Illinois State Police, for example, have fostered a culture of severe disapproval for law officers' stretching the truth.

Yet there is a fundamental tension between the law on one hand and the police on the other. Cops tend to judge themselves according to one criterion, their success in performing the job we demand of them: protecting us. The law wants more—it wants the cops to catch bad guys, all right, but it wants them to do it fairly, with convincing evidence that they have gathered while respecting the minimal standards of decency we call "rights."

Thus it falls to the courts and lawyers to insist on strict adherence to all those rules that the police often regard as a pesky hindrance. And unfortunately, some prosecutors and judges too often seem willing to look the other way when an officer's testimony just doesn't add up.

I first realized that the L.A.P.D. was in deep trouble during an early hearing in the O.J. Simpson case. Detectives testified that they had gone over a wall and into Mr. Simpson's house without a search warrant because they had been afraid that Mr. Simpson and others were in danger. Anyone with experience in the criminal justice system would have strongly suspected that the officers' most likely motive had been a zeal to question Mr. Simpson before he hired a lawyer. What shocked me was not that the cops offered this dubious justification, but that the Los Angeles County prosecutors had put them on the stand—on national television, no less—to testify to it, and that the judge accepted the officers' statements as admissible.

That is why I'm not confident that the Los Angeles district attorney, Gil Garcetti, can conduct a fully independent investigation of the misdeeds of the cops there. I was not comforted when the city decided last week to let the police department and prosecutors' office continue their investigations with no outside oversight.

There are prosecutors—New York City's Robert Morgenthau is usually held up as the example—who are constantly at odds with their police departments because of their refusal to tolerate breaking the rules. Mr. Garcetti has yet to prove he belongs in that group.

Prosecutors anywhere who are willing to let police officers do whatever they have to in order to convict may soon find themselves dealing with cops who do whatever they want.

Few Police Officers Are Corrupt

Al Martinez

Al Martinez is a columnist for the Los Angeles Times.

Police officers who are caught breaking the law are big news stories, but the number of "dirty" police officers is miniscule compared to the number of police officers who are willing to risk their lives to help the public remain safe. Just as there are cases of police misconduct, there are examples of police officers who died during the performance of their duty. The public should not think that all police officers are corrupt.

Editor's note: About seventy Los Angeles police officers have been implicated in various forms of misconduct in the Rampart scandal. Eight Rampart officers have been charged with crimes, and more than one hundred criminal convictions have been overturned due to police misconduct.

There's nothing in society more odious than good guys going bad.
We're a culture reared on being saved at the last minute either by a knight, the cavalry or someone responding to 911.

We revere the gun-totin' marshal who cleans up the Old West, and the army that marches in to show some tyrant a thing or two.

We love good guys. And when the good guys reveal a darker side, the moral ground we've always trod upon seems to suddenly give way.

That's the way L.A. is feeling today.

Cops as thugs and thieves

Our cops have suddenly become not the guardians of social order, but thugs and thieves. We feel betrayed and vulnerable. I hear it on the street and in my telephone messages. I see it in my e-mail.

Those who love cops mourn. Those who hate cops chortle. It's best to neither a lover nor a hater be. That's where I stand.

What I see is the possibility of maybe a dozen members of the LAPD who could be "dirty" in the sense that they might have squandered a public trust. Given guns and uniforms, they've used them, says a fallen cop, against us.

These are the words of Rafael Perez, caught with his fingers in the cookie, I mean *cokie,* jar and now singing like a cockatiel to cut a deal for himself.

The song he offers is about cops involved in illegal shootings, beatings, shakedowns and evidence planting. It's the worst kind of song for a department already under investigation for recent cases of brutality and bad judgment.

But don't start forming a vigilante committee just yet.

The good and the bad

What we have here, you see, is maybe a dozen out of about 10,000 members of the LAPD who might've turned rotten. And maybe there are a dozen more or even a hundred more we don't know about. But there are still all those others who will risk their lives to save ours.

They're the ones I'm writing about today.

Anyone who reads my columns knows that I'm not an apologist for cops. I've been around too long to play that game.

I've written about tainted badges in L.A., Long Beach, Riverside, San Bernardino, Claremont, El Monte and in other places I can't even remember.

I've also written about cops who have stopped bullets in the performance of their duty and in adherence to their moral commitment.

There've been 191 L.A. officers killed in the last 50 years, including 17 in the last 10. The most recent was Brian Brown, a young, dedicated guy who wanted to do what was right for the people. He was gunned down by a gang member last December trying to catch a killer.

What we have here . . . is maybe a dozen out of about 10,000 members of the LAPD who might've turned rotten.

I remember television images of his 7-year-old son, Dylon, staring straight ahead as his father, an only parent, was buried. I remember him saying, "I love my dad and will miss him." The memory of that boy continues to claw at the heart.

It wasn't Brown the policeman then. It was a kid's father.

And there was Filbert Cuesta that same year, and Steve Gajda. Before that, Joe Rios and David Schmid and Christy Hamilton and Raymond Messerly and Charles Champe and Tina Kerbrat.

So many, so young, so selfless.

I know, there was Margaret Mitchell too, the fragile, mentally ill woman holding a screwdriver who was killed by a cop; Daniel Zarraga, armed with nothing more than a ballpoint pen, shot down by a cop; and Efrain Lopez, waving a broomstick handle, brought down with nine bullets fired by a cop. And more.

The LAPD hadn't been in a position of such low esteem since the days of Daryl Gates and the beating of Rodney King . . . until we began hearing sordid tales of the alleged dirty dozen who had sold their honor for money and for tarnished glory.

And down went esteem another notch.

What happens now? We all know this is no time for the kind of "internal review" that cops love. Closed doors hide too many secrets. Whispers conceal unpleasant truths.

So everyone but the Mormon Tabernacle Choir is investigating the charges made by Rafael Perez. If the charges are true, we've got some rotten ones to deal with all right. If they're false, God help Perez.

This is not a terrific time for L.A. Our social structure has been undermined at a critical juncture in our history. The good guys are in question. But even the worst crisis is eventually resolved. Hopefully, justice will prevail in this case and we can move on to other issues, other scandals, other indecencies. Everything passes. Life rolls forward.

But I can't help thinking back to a veteran street cop who resigned in 1991 because of the Rodney King beating.

He looked at me and said, "We aren't all that way."

I know.

10

Critics Exaggerate the Problem of Police Corruption

Joseph Wambaugh

Joseph Wambaugh, the author of numerous crime and police books, was a policeman in the Los Angeles Police Department for fourteen years.

Critics of the police erroneously allege that police departments are awash in corruption and need external oversight. However, during the corruption scandal in the Rampart division of the Los Angeles Police Department (LAPD), it was the LAPD that caught the rogue officer whose confession started the investigation. It was also the Los Angeles Police Department that verified the officer's allegations of misconduct. Furthermore, despite all the scandal, relatively few officers have been charged with serious crimes. Unfortunately, the LAPD will most likely use draconian tactics while investigating the wrongdoing in an effort to convince critics that the department can police itself.

The Los Angeles Police Department (LAPD) has been rocked by allegations of massive illegalities centered in its gang-plagued Rampart Division. At least 21 officers have either left the force or been placed on suspension pending investigation of charges that cops planted evidence, intimidated witnesses, and covered up unjustified shootings and beatings. At least 40 criminal convictions have already been overturned, and many more may be. . . . Rafael Perez, the rogue cop whose confession kicked off this scandal, was sentenced to five years in prison for stealing eight pounds of cocaine.

An outstanding job

Guess who caught Mr. Perez? The LAPD, that's who. And guess who immediately turned on the afterburners and sent 50 investigators to just about every prison in California and beyond to check out the allegations?

You guessed it. Yet if you read the headlines you might think the LAPD is awash in corruption and out of control, à la *L.A. Confidential,* that popular piece of cinematic fiction based on James Ellroy's overheated novel.

Internal Affairs Investigators . . . can search cops' homes without benefit of warrants and interrogate them without benefit of lawyers.

You only have to tune in to a Geraldo Rivera show to catch the likes of supersnide attorney Alan Dershowitz (notorious in cop circles for his demonstrably preposterous claim that cops are trained in "testilying" [lying in court]) in order to hear gleeful predictions that the Rampart scandal will result in the release of "thousands" of the wrongly convicted.

Here we go again. The same attempt to vilify the LAPD was made after the Rodney King incident, an extraordinarily aberrant example of very excessive force directed by a police sergeant intent on making an ex-convict cry "uncle." The Rodney King affair resulted in the hiring of an outsider, Chief Willie Williams of Philadelphia, to "clean up" the LAPD. A few years later Mr. Williams was hastily bought out of his contract by the city fathers, who realized that he was hopelessly out of his depth. That led to the elevation of our present chief, Bernard Parks, a seasoned LAPD veteran.

Chief Parks is not out of his depth. In fact, one could hardly imagine a more perfect administrator to handle this scandal: He is intelligent, articulate, educated and (a relevant fact in a racially divided city) African-American. What should be most reassuring to critics, he's a rigid disciplinarian. In fact, the Los Angeles Police Protective League—the police union—sneeringly refers to him as "Burnie" Parks because of his penchant for remorselessly roasting cops for minor infractions. In a public attempt to embarrass Chief Parks, some LAPD cops requested through the media that he not attend their funerals if they are killed in the line of duty.

Alas, police critics are never satisfied, and they have demanded an "outside" investigation of the Rampart scandal. . . . The Justice Department assigned six special agents from the Federal Bureau of Investigation to oversee the Rampart investigation and report any violations of civil rights. Some call it window dressing, but perhaps it's good dressing in that the FBI has cachet and might reassure a suspicious public.

But these feds cannot match the ruthlessly effective tactics of LAPD Internal Affairs investigators, who can search cops' homes without benefit of warrants and interrogate them without benefit of lawyers. If cops insist on their Constitutional rights, they can be fired for insubordination. No suspect has as few rights as a cop under investigation by Internal Affairs.

Predictions

With the FBI on the scene, perhaps critics will simmer down and let the investigation proceed without calling for indictments every hour or so. But I predict they will not.

Speaking of predictions, I made one on "Larry King Live" during the early stage of the O.J. Simpson trial. [Simpson was charged with murdering his ex-wife and her companion in 1995.] Taking into account the racial and gender makeup of the jury, and Mr. Simpson's icon status in the African-American community, I predicted that he would be acquitted and subsequently serve as grand marshal in Pasadena's Tournament of Roses Parade. I got the second part wrong.

I herewith offer another prediction, this one about the Rampart scandal. I predict that scores of cops will be charged with minor infractions unrelated to any criminal activity, but there will be draconian suspensions and pay losses, which will make many families suffer. And there will only be a handful of criminal cops charged with serious felonies. Those few cops will be convicted. None will ever ride in a Rose Parade.

11

Corrupt Police Officers Are Often Heroes

Erica Werner and Paul Chavez

Erica Werner and Paul Chavez are reporters for the Times Union *newspaper in Albany, New York.*

In 1998 it was discovered that many officers in the Los Angeles Police Department (LAPD) framed innocent people for crimes they did not commit, perjured themselves to help get convictions, and participated in or covered up such crimes as theft, drug dealing, and even murder. Many officers—and some neighborhood residents—believed that these actions were justifiable because they helped reduce the area's crime rate. The residents have been reluctant to condemn the corrupt police officers because the corruption made the neighborhood's streets safer than they have been for years. While some neighborhood residents see the scandal as involving just a few "bad apples," others are bitter about their treatment from the police.

On a warm summer afternoon along the streets of one of Los Angeles' toughest neighborhoods, Bertha Wooldridge began the daily ritual of shutting down her narrow hardware store, hoping to make it home with a few hours left of daylight.

But as she tidied up, four teen-age gang members burst through the still-unlocked door. They were nervous, unsure. They looked like children, and yet the violence they threatened made them seem adults.

They forced Wooldridge to her knees with a gun to her head. They yanked off the gold wedding ring her husband bought 14 years earlier. They threatened to kill her two employees.

"Everybody asked me, 'Were you afraid? Were you afraid?' But I was mad," said Wooldridge, a Mexican immigrant who has run her store in the neighborhood called Rampart for two decades. "These people think they can get away with it."

Her ordeal ended better than many: Police showed up and chased the young robbers off. They captured two without firing a shot.

Saviors and enemies

Since that day, Wooldridge has treated the embattled Los Angeles Police Department like saviors. And that includes the cops of the Rampart Station, at the center of the worst corruption scandal in the city's history.

Those same cops are the enemy for George Torres.

A member of the fast-growing Mara Salvatrucha gang, the 21-year-old Torres said he was busted for drug possession in March 1998 after police planted $10 of crack cocaine on him, a charge heard often in the Rampart scandal.

In several cases, prosecutors have concluded such corruption claims were true.

Torres said he and a fellow gang member were defending their "turf," chasing away two trespassers—who turned out to be undercover cops. No, said police in their report: Torres walked up to their car and offered to sell them drugs.

Torres pleaded no contest and accepted a one-year county jail sentence. But prosecutors now say his case could be re-examined as part of the corruption probe.

Wearing a baseball cap pulled low to hide gang tattoos on his forehead, Torres talked of his life and his run-ins with police.

His mother died of cancer while he was locked up. His final promise to her was that he would abandon life on the street. He's trying, he insisted. "If I had the chance, I'd go to school and change my life."

In a city accustomed to tales of police abuse, the alleged misdeeds of the Rampart Station's anti-gang unit still have the power to shock. The first reports emerged [in the fall of 1999]. Today, the alleged abuses read like a how-to for disregarding laws that limit power and authority—planting evidence, lying under oath and beating, framing and shooting innocent people.

Judges have overturned more than 90 convictions, the police department has fired, suspended or relieved of duty more than 30 officers, and four policemen face criminal charges as the investigation continues.

Yet, Rampart has caused little outcry from political leaders in the nation's second-largest city.

Nobody supports what [the police] did. But the results were good for the neighborhood.

The LAPD's Rampart Station—named for a street that bisects the neighborhood—covers 7.9 crime-ridden square miles just west of downtown. The area is populated largely by newly arrived Central American and Mexican immigrants, a large share of whom crowd into one-bedroom apartments and work two jobs to make ends meet.

Many fear both the police and the gangs the cops target.

As immigrants in a city uneasy with its diversity, residents are wary of speaking up. And yet some do complain about police misconduct, increasingly since the scandal broke. At the same time, many are reluctant to condemn the officers who have made their streets dramatically safer in recent years.

In 1992, the worst year for gang violence in Los Angeles, Rampart led the city with 149 homicides. By 1998, 34 homicides were reported in the precinct. [In 1999] there were 32. Crime, however, is on the rise citywide, with 19 homicides reported in Rampart [as of July 2000]—a bump that police strongly hint is a repercussion of the low morale and dismissals that resulted from the corruption probe.

"People are really torn," said Adolfo V. Nodal, former general manager of Los Angeles' Cultural Affairs Department, and a resident of Rampart since 1983. "Nobody supports what they did. But the results were good for the neighborhood."

But Wooldridge and Torres capture Rampart's shades of gray.

Deterioration and renewal

A native of Chihuahua, Mexico, who never lost her accent, Wooldridge owns Westlake Plumbing and Hardware with her husband, Robert.

The store, crowded from floor to ceiling with paint thinner, potpourri, tools and other merchandise, is in the middle of the Rampart district, a few blocks from MacArthur Park.

A hundred years ago this was a fashionable neighborhood of hotels, theaters and stores. The area began to deteriorate in the 1970s, as the city's upscale neighborhoods marched west. With the crack epidemic of the late 1980s, crime got so bad that corpses were occasionally fished from the lake and residents refused to venture there even in daylight.

Since the police crackdown of the past five years, locals have seen a pronounced decrease in gang activity and graffiti. Although gang members and the homeless still congregate in MacArthur Park, now plenty of families are there, too, along with couples, kids kicking soccer balls and workers on their lunch breaks.

In the years when crime was bad, Wooldridge's store was broken into 19 times, she said, patting the stack of police reports that even today are tucked under her counter as a reminder. The time in 1991 when gang members held her at gunpoint was the final straw.

Wooldridge, 52, who wears an LAPD lapel pin on her white sweater, became a crime fighter. She got involved in neighborhood watches, was host to police-community meetings and occasionally helped translate.

"Let's face it—the police are your protection," she said. "Either we had to close the store or fight back."

Wooldridge said she wants to protect her neighborhood, and she sees the Rampart scandal as nothing more than the work of a few bad apples.

The LAPD, however, has long had a tense relationship with the Hispanic community, from the "zoot suit riots" of 1943, when police stood by as marauding U.S. servicemen attacked Hispanic youths, to the Bloody Christmas scandal a few years later, when the jailhouse beatings of seven Hispanics led to the first indictments of active LAPD officers.

It's tension well known to Torres, who remains bitter about his treatment by police.

Torres spends his free time hanging out on Francis Street, a two-block strip of gated apartment buildings near a main boulevard filled with stalls offering Hispanic fare such as Salvadoran pupusa and fast-food joints selling Korean barbecue.

Mara Salvatrucha gang members send mixed messages on the street: All appears innocent when they run around playfully dousing each other with water on a hot afternoon; but they also deal marijuana and cocaine here.

Torres is one of the most recent victims of the violence.

Shortly after speaking with the Associated Press, he attended a party in nearby Echo Park. Later that night, as Torres was riding his bike on Francis Street, a gunman approached him and opened fire. A bullet struck Torres in the head, leaving him a quadriplegic.

Rampart police are looking for suspects.

12

Federal Oversight of Police Departments Is Reducing Police Misconduct

Steven H. Rosenbaum

Steven H. Rosenbaum is the head of the special litigation section of the Civil Rights Division of the U.S. Department of Justice.

Trust between the public and police has eroded because of the perception that police are too aggressive, biased, and disrespectful toward the citizens they are sworn to protect. However, by increasing the enforcement of people's civil rights, police integrity can be improved and police misconduct eliminated. When "a pattern or practice" of civil rights violations has been observed in a police department, the Department of Justice can intervene and require police departments to institute better training, supervisory, management, and disciplinary programs. These programs have been very successful in reducing police misconduct. As instances of police misconduct decline, public trust in the police—an important element in fighting crime—increases.

Attorney General Janet Reno spoke about how police officers do their jobs. Let me share with you some of her eloquent words:

> Police officers have one of the hardest jobs there is. A police officer is charged with ensuring public safety, but she or he is also empowered to use force and, if necessary, to take a life to protect others from death or great bodily harm. The police are there to protect us from crime, but they must protect our rights at the same time. And to do their work effectively, the police must have the trust and confidence of the communities they serve. They must develop a partnership and a relationship with the citizens they protect.
>
> Professional, sensitive, and dedicated police officers have done so much across this country to make their community

From Steven H. Rosenbaum's statement before the National Association of Police Organizations' National Law Enforcement Rights Center Legal Rights and Legislative Seminar in Washington, D.C., April 26, 1999.

a far better place to live. In many communities police and citizens are working together to prevent crime and to build understanding and to bring people together.

The crime rate has fallen every year for the past six years in virtually every category. Policing has contributed to that drop. The thousands of community-oriented police officers who are on the streets, due to President Bill Clinton's COPS [Community-Oriented Policing Services] initiative, have made a difference. All across America neighborhoods are safer.

But some people, especially those in minority communities, are wondering whether our success in reducing crime has been due in part to overly aggressive police officers who ignore the civil liberties of Americans. . . . The issue is national in scope and reaches people all across this country. For too many people . . . the trust that is so essential to effective policing does not exist because residents believe that police have used excessive force, that law enforcement is too aggressive, that law enforcement is biased, disrespectful, and unfair.

Five areas of reform

The Attorney General identified five areas that "will form the foundation of [the] efforts to foster police integrity and eliminate police misconduct." They are:

1. "Expand and promote the kind of partnership and dialogue which develops the mutual trust and confidence between police and the people they serve";
2. "Insist on police accountability";
3. "Ensure that police departments recruit officers who reflect the communities they serve, who have high standards and who are then properly trained to deal with the stresses and the dangers of police work";
4. "Increase [federal] civil rights enforcement," and
5. "Take steps to gather the data that will help define the scope of the problem and measure our efforts to solve it."

She has defined a large and significant task. To succeed, it will require the dedication and commitment of those in law enforcement: police chiefs and managers working together with rank and file officers and the unions that represent them. And it will need support and contributions from community leaders and civil rights advocates who want to be part of the solution. That is why the Attorney General will be convening representatives of these groups and experts in police practices "to identify and share strategies that are working and to understand suggestions that can be implemented."

Civil rights enforcement program

We have our work cut out for us. As the Attorney General's remarks suggest, there are many aspects of the Justice Department's program for combating police misconduct. What I have been asked to talk about to-day is the Department's civil [rights] enforcement program. We are doing very important work, and welcome your attention to it.

When Rodney King was brutally beaten by police officers [in Los An-geles in 1991], the Justice Department had the power to bring criminal prosecutions against those officers. And we did—successfully prosecuting two of them. But we did not have the power to reform management prac-tices of law enforcement agencies that countenanced such misconduct. In 1994, Congress recognized this deficiency and filled the void.

As part of the Violent Crime Control and Law Enforcement Act of 1994, the same statute that created the COPS program, Congress autho-rized the Department of Justice to file lawsuits to eliminate a "pattern or practice" of conduct by law enforcement officers that violates federal civil rights. 42 U.S.C. 14141. The statute's reach is very broad and so is our en-forcement program. Examples of the types of systemic problems we ad-dress are: excessive force; improper searches; false arrests; discriminatory harassment, stops, searches, or arrests; and retaliation against persons al-leging misconduct.

The great majority of police officers in America perform their enormously difficult job with professionalism, integrity, and respect for the rights of civilians.

Two older statutes, Title VI of the Civil Rights Act of 1964, 42 U.S.C. 2000d, and the Omnibus Crime Control and Safe Streets Act of 1968, 42 U.S.C. 3789d, together prohibit police departments receiving federal fi-nancial assistance from discriminating on the basis of race, color, na-tional origin and religion in providing police services. Under these laws, the Justice Department can, among other things, initiate administrative investigations based upon complaints from individuals.

I will, however, focus my remarks on our new "pattern or practice" au-thority. Now that we have a congressional mandate, we have launched "pattern or practice" investigations in jurisdictions in which we have seen sufficient preliminary evidence of a systemic problem to warrant a closer look. In deciding whether to open an investigation, we gather information from a variety of sources, including federal and state prosecutors, criminal investigations or prosecutions of police officers, civil litigation, individual or organizational complaints, investigative reports of governmental or other bodies and accounts in the news media. A "pattern or practice" in-vestigation may be launched only after the recommendation is reviewed and approved by the head of the Civil Rights Division.

Long-standing Department practice prevents me from discussing the specifics of any ongoing investigation. But I can tell you that all types of law enforcement agencies are involved—large and small; urban, suburban, and rural. Our investigations are independent, thorough, and fair. As a general matter, the agencies we investigate have cooperated willingly with us. Indeed . . . the Mayor and Chief of Police of the District of Columbia asked us to conduct an investigation of the police department's use of force—an invitation we were pleased to receive and pleased to accept.

There are solutions to the problem of police misconduct, solutions that will aid not just the civil rights of civilians, but the effectiveness of policing.

These are not simple investigations. The exercise of our pattern or practice authority must be based on competent, concrete evidence of systemic problems of great magnitude. Our investigations and our lawsuits are very different from criminal investigations and prosecutions. Our focus is management, not just the alleged bad conduct by problem officers.

Consent decrees

So far, we have filed two lawsuits against municipal police departments seeking to remedy a pattern or practice of misconduct. Our first suit involved the Pittsburgh, Pennsylvania Bureau of Police and the second involved the Steubenville, Ohio Police Department. (*United States* v. *City of Pittsburgh . . .* and *United States* v. *City of Steubenville . . .*). In each, we were able to settle our claims by way of a consent decree—an agreement of the parties entered as an enforceable court order by a federal district judge. Both consent decrees establish mandatory guidelines for the training, supervision and discipline of police officers, as well as receiving, investigating and responding to civilian complaints of misconduct. Both decrees have been implemented without violating existing collective bargaining agreements or impairing collective bargaining rights. We are proud that the decrees are already being used as models of "best practices."

We are finding that where a department has systemic problems, management systems exist that could help better train, supervise, monitor and discipline its officers. What we try to do in our cases is require implementation of these kinds of systems. For example, where a city has had many incidents in which officers have used excessive force, we would require the city to train its officers in proper techniques for avoiding and overcoming resistance, so that force is used only when necessary and only in appropriate ways. Where problem officers have escaped oversight or discipline for civil rights violations, we would require a comprehensive monitoring and supervisory system. Where civilians' complaints have gone uninvestigated, we would require improved procedures and policies governing internal affairs investigations. Or where stops, searches, or seizures are improperly based on race or ethnic origin, we would require auditing, training, and correction of police officers who engage in this discriminatory behavior.

These kinds of reforms work. Let me tell you about Steubenville, one of the departments covered by a consent decree with us. The department, with about 50 officers, had been plagued with civil rights problems for years—reflected in nearly 60 lawsuits that cost the city about $870,000 in claims. About 18 months after entry of the decree, the City Attorney reported that for the first time in 23 years there were no pending lawsuits against the police department. In his words: "We're really beginning to see the benefits of the consent decree."

We know that the great majority of police officers in America perform their enormously difficult job with professionalism, integrity, and respect for the rights of civilians. But police managers must train officers, monitor them, supervise them and, where necessary, discipline them. Good officers need training and assistance in dealing with the enormous pressures of their jobs. Potentially problem officers need help and correction—*before* they violate civil rights. And bad officers need to be disciplined and even fired, when necessary. The key is accountability.

The managerial tasks I have outlined can have enormous impact not just on civil rights abuses, but on effective crime-fighting. As Attorney General Reno noted, a bedrock principle of effective law enforcement is community support for the work of the police. Few things undermine that support as much as the perception that the police are abusing their power with impunity. Solve the problem leading to the perception, and you enlist community support for the police. We are confident our enforcement of the 1994 statute serves that goal. There are solutions to the problem of police misconduct, solutions that will aid not just the civil rights of civilians, but the effectiveness of policing.

We are fortunate today because the nation is paying attention to issues of police integrity and effectiveness. Managing police departments has been and will remain primarily the task of state and local law enforcement agencies. Our approach, therefore, is one of respect for, and appreciation of, efforts being made at the state and local level to enforce high standards of integrity and constitutional conduct among officers. Our goal is to ensure that those who enforce the law respect the rights of every person. We share the task of reaching this goal with the officers, themselves, as well as with those in local and state government and in the community. We firmly believe, working together, this is a goal we can and should achieve.

13

Corrupt Police Departments Are Difficult to Reform

Eric Monkkonen

Eric Monkkonen, a leading crime historian, is a professor of history and policy studies at the University of California, Los Angeles.

The first response to a major scandal in a police department is to establish a commission to investigate the problem and recommend solutions. However, the commissions' recommendations usually do not end corruption because they are rarely followed unless laws are passed requiring police departments to make the suggested changes. In addition, police officers have little training compared to other professionals, but a great deal of power, responsibility, and individual discretion. All these factors come together to contribute to unpredictable outcomes in policing. While commissions and their recommendations are better than doing nothing to resolve a department's problems, they seldom produce any lasting changes.

P olice corruption is nearly as old as policing. The current scandal roiling the Los Angeles Police Department, though it may have some slightly different twists, is not unique. [Many officers within the Rampart division of the LAPD were accused by another officer of corruption, including perjury, planting evidence, and stealing drugs.] There is even a historic pattern in the public response to such scandals: the hope that a commission of esteemed notables can investigate the incidents and cure the problem.

Two kinds of corruption

There have been two kinds of police corruption. The first, and ultimately the worst, is between the police and the political process, in which cops influence elections and political parties control access to police jobs. Police, in turn, look the other way at electoral misbehavior. This sort of corruption strikes at the core of democratic political systems but describes

From "The Problem with Commissions," by Eric Monkkonen, *Los Angeles Times*, September 26, 1999. Copyright © 1999 by The Los Angeles Times Syndicate. Reprinted with permission.

the situations in many 19th- and early-20th-century U.S. cities, where political corruption was a major problem.

The current LAPD crisis is an example of the second type of corruption: between police and criminal offenders, not their victims. Police officers allegedly victimized gang members, some of whom may have been criminal offenders. Prosecuting gang members is difficult, because their victims are often other gang members. They are reluctant witnesses, afraid of reprisals and perhaps as opposed to the police as to other gangsters. So police may fabricate evidence or lie in court—in New York City, in the 1990s, police officers called it "testilying." A bad practice that began with ends justifying means can turn into corruption for profit instead of corruption for crime control.

In general, this second kind of corruption depends on the nature of vice, which has no complaining victims or outside parties to participate in the relationship between police and offenders. When a police officer arrests a person for prostitution or selling drugs, credibility is on the officer's side, making it easy for the officer to lie and difficult for the offender to complain: Whom is the jury going to believe? If the "victims" of vice—dope dealers' or prostitutes' customers—were willing to complain and testify, vice control would be easier and the police would be in a poor position to lie.

The problem with these ad hoc groups is that they have little clout unless their recommendations are followed up by legislative action.

New York City has been visible as a leader in many things good and bad. The tight connection between the police and the Tammany Hall political machine lingered into the 20th century. Political parties arranged for men to get policing jobs, ensuring their allegiance. Starting in the mid-19th century, the link involved both vice and politics. Here's how it worked: Police officers collected payoffs from illegal vice or after-hours operations, in turn ignoring or going easy on illegal activities. Some of the money went into the political parties, some made officers rich. By the 1890s, there were officers like Alexander "Clubber" Williams, who policed the vice district in New York City. On a policeman's salary, he managed to acquire an estate in Connecticut and a steam launch.

Creating an investigative commission

When public awareness of scandal comes to a boil, there is a traditionally accepted response: Create a commission to investigate. Composed of important people, commissions meet for a discrete purpose, take witness testimony, issue reports and disband. Los Angeles has had many, most recently the Christopher Commission in 1991 [which investigated allegations of police brutality following the beating of Rodney King]. But the problem with these ad hoc groups is that they have little clout unless their recommendations are followed up by legislative action.

Why so little impact, given the prestige and expertise they command? Because the commissions are not stakeholders in the process; they do not live with the consequences of their recommendations. Their careers are not on the line, nor do they have continuing involvement.

Just because there is a pattern to police corruption does not mean there is a standard way to deal with it.

Historically, two investigative commissions achieved particular notoriety. The first was prompted by a city so corrupt that no agency had the power and independence to investigate its police: the 1894 Lexow committee of New York state, which investigated police corruption in New York City. This investigation, while looking into real problems, was motivated by a Republican legislature seeking to gain control of Democratic New York City. This does not diminish the commission's portrait of police corruption: how politicians used police to extract money from vice and to keep control of the polls. The police had become a direct part of the machinery used by political parties to stay in power. Though the Democrats lost the mayor's office as a result, historian James Richardson concludes the resulting reforms were "not very impressive."

The second important committee was the 1929 Wickersham Commission, which examined crime and criminal justice in the nation. Initiated during President Herbert Hoover's administration, the commission produced a high-quality 14-volume report. One volume dealt with police corruption, abuse and torture of prisoners (euphemistically called the "third degree"). Its title gets the point across: "Report on Lawlessness in Law Enforcement." But by the time of its publication in 1931, the country was in the Great Depression, which distracted the nation's attention from its criminal-justice system.

The morals of this commission's story: One, what happens after an event can completely alter its meaning and impact; and, two, police reform has frustrated some of the nation's best minds.

Corruption in Los Angeles

Somewhat earlier than the national Wickersham Commission, the Crime Commission of Los Angeles tried to clean up L.A.'s corrupt police department by hiring Berkeley's August Vollmer as a reform chief in 1923. All too effective, he lasted only one year. Vollmer attempted to apply the best "scientific" thinking to policing by convening a conference of police executives and university professors. The effort resulted in a report that, according to Joseph G. Woods, was the only such report since 1897 that the City Council filed and refused to publish. Published by Woods 50 years later, the report revealed that the LAPD's racism, intolerance and ineffectiveness mirrored that of the larger society. Woods concludes that in "1924, August Vollmer was too advanced for Los Angeles, or any other American city. Police reform stopped when he left." The report contained Vollmer's recommendations for reorganizing the police. It is now best read as an example of how difficult it is to get much useful thinking about policing.

In the 1930s, L.A. officers were linked to the corrupt Mayor Frank L.

Shaw in a manner similar to their counterparts in New York, with one major exception. Control of the electoral process was no longer operative. But Depression Los Angeles saw severe police corruption. The postwar reforms initiated by Chief William H. Parker were significant, creating a department that prided itself on its lack of political corruption. It is important to remember it has remained free of this taint.

Just because there is a pattern to police corruption does not mean there is a standard way to deal with it. Exhortation, investigation, better training and higher standards are all good ideas. But the fundamental fact is, police are in an odd situation: For the most part, they are not independently trained professionals, like doctors or lawyers, yet they have enormous power and responsibility. (The highly rated Los Angeles Police Academy is a seven-month program.) They are asked to make difficult decisions. Even in the best of times, there is not an exact guide to behavior for police officers, so individual discretion adds up to hard-to-control outcomes.

At the end of the 20th century, the U.S. has achieved honest electoral processes, free from police influence. This is an important gain. But it is not enough.

Troubled relations

The often troubled relation between police and the public remains. Vice, as most police managers know, is always a potential source of officer misbehavior and corruption. Police abuse of individuals when there are no outside witnesses is hard to monitor. No one solution can be relied on. Police problems may be predictable, but solutions are not. Oversight agencies, whether internal or external, can help, but cannot substitute for internal demands for fairness, honesty and quality.

On the other hand, as with similar organizations, schools, for example, the tone is set at the top. Police executives can demand quality, but if those who hire chiefs and control budgets do not make this clear, the city has little reason to expect it. If the city's message is, "Stop the gangs, we don't care how," then it has to accept responsibility for its agents.

Commissions, whether internal or external, are better than complacency. One hundred years after the first such commission, and the modest shake-up it caused, it is hard to believe any oversight investigation can produce lasting structural change. Different versions of old problems constantly emerge. This should not cause us to disparage the work that will go into investigating and trying to fix the current crisis, but it should serve as a cautionary tale. Policing change comes with difficulty, that we know for sure.

14

The Public Must Protest Police Corruption

Kelly Sarabyn

Kelly Sarabyn is a columnist for the University of Virginia's newspaper,
the Cavalier Daily.

Police corruption is a serious problem for society, yet Americans
do not rise up in protest over the latest revelations of police
wrongdoing. People give many excuses for their inaction over police corruption, but the real reason is that they are selfish. As long
as police corruption is directed toward poor minorities, middle-
and upper-class Americans will continue to allow innocent people
to be abused by police.

Your new name is 73645. Your new room is Cell Block 386. And your
new roommate is a convicted rapist. You can have all this, and more,
courtesy of the Los Angeles Police Department.

But wait, you say, don't I need to commit a crime to receive this won-
derful prize package?

The answer, of course, should be yes. But in the case of the LAPD (Los
Angeles Police Department), and a growing number of police departments across the nation, the answer is a surprising no.

Four officers in the Los Angeles Police Department stand accused of
lying, fabricating evidence, and falsifying police records in order to "send
innocent men to jail," according to the *Washington Post*.

This incident epitomizes the corruption that has flooded through the
pearly gates of our criminal justice system. Racial profiling, police beatings and sleepy public defenders have all become regular facets of American justice.

An unacceptable silence

The majority of Americans would agree this is a problem. A huge problem. Yet the incident in California, and many other recent ones, have

provoked no public indignation. No protest rallies. No overflow of letters in the Congressional mailbox.

This silence is unacceptable.

Society needs to stop making excuses, and realize the criminal justice system is not going to fix itself. Citizens often think the justice system is not under their control, and consequentially they cannot change its operations. There are no public elections for police officers. Judges usually are appointed. Police departments are sprawling bureaucracies with lives of their own.

These facts are true, but it does not mean the public does not have power over the justice system. Ultimately, all governmental appointments can be traced back to an elected official.

People can write their representative or governor and let elected officials know corruption is an issue. Representatives can enact legislation that provides for checks on police abuse. Governors can appoint judges who are strong advocates of procedural rights.

Elected officials can enforce responsibility. Elected officials only will do this, however, if they know the issue is important to their constituents. It is the responsibility of the people to make their interests known.

Another excuse people use to justify their inaction is the claim that police abuses are unfortunate, but inevitable accompaniments to any justice system. Officers are, after all, humans. We cannot expect humans to be perfect.

This is also true. We should not expect our officers to be perfect. Errors made in good faith and judgment are tolerable. We should not, however, stand for intentional procedural abuses. Police who toss aside the truth in order to bolster their conviction rate have not erred. They have deliberately broken the law.

The main reason for the public's inaction, however, is not a consideration for the moral fallibility of police officers. It is pure selfishness. The abuses of the criminal justice system are directed at one demographic—poor minorities. The LAPD incident occurred within their Rampart Division—a unit that operates in a neighborhood of lower class immigrants.

Middle- and upper-class citizens generally do not have to worry about police officers planting drugs in their cars. Nor do they have to worry about inept public defenders botching their cases.

Most people, in fact, can rest assured that they will not be wrongly imprisoned. The problem of police corruption is therefore neither a pressing concern, nor an issue for public outrage. There are numerous reasons, however, why it should be a pressing concern for all citizens, and not just the citizens who are targeted.

Justice should be blind. Innocent men should be free. Police are supposed to protect and serve. Poor minorities have few political or economic resources in which to respond to the abuses.

Americans pride themselves on living in the land of the free. Yet, citizens sit idly by, watching as the government robs citizens of their freedom.

Corrupt police officers are imprisoning innocent people. You are paying their salaries. You are involved. Stop deflecting responsibility. Speak out on behalf of those who do not have the resources to be heard.

15

Personality Tests Do Not Indicate the Potential for Corruption

Jennifer O'Connor Boes, Callie J. Chandler, and Howard W. Timm

Jennifer O'Connor Boes and Callie J. Chandler research personnel and security issues for the BDM Federal Corporation; Howard W. Timm is a research psychologist who investigates personnel security and violence issues for the Defense Personnel Security Research Center in Monterey, California.

Personality tests used by police departments to identify police recruits who may be prone to becoming corrupt have been found to be ineffective. However, there are traits that were common in those who did participate in police corruption (known as "violators.") Violators were found to have more difficulty getting along with other people, they often disregarded society's rules and laws, and were frequently immature, unreliable, and irresponsible. But perhaps the best way to predict if a police officer would become corrupt is if the officer engaged in other types of misconduct after being hired by the police department.

The primary research question addressed in this study of police betrayal is whether pre-employment psychological screening tests can identify individuals prone to engage in acts of trust betrayal. And, by inference, whether a similar method be developed to screen out people who might be prone to commit espionage.

We posed the question as part of our study of espionage, a subject of great concern to the Defense Personnel Security Research Center (PERSEREC). The major problem in studying espionage, however, is that it occurs relatively rarely. Thus, only a few cases become available for analysis. On the other hand, similar acts of betrayal do occur in other contexts: people sometimes embezzle money, and some law enforcement officers commit acts of betrayal (serious crimes). If we could increase the numbers of cases of such espionage-like betrayal in our databases and thus be able to conduct statistically meaningful analyses, our work could lead to an enhanced understanding of why some people, including spies, commit acts of trust betrayal.

In this study, we used police corruption as the surrogate for espionage. Policemen, and those with access to government secrets, are all required to submit to thorough background checks before being employed. However, in the case of the police, many are given personality tests as part of their standard pre-employment screening battery. By examining the test materials filled out during the job application process and comparing them to the records of policemen who later commit crimes, our researchers attempted to answer the question of whether the pre-employment tests could be used to identify, and even perhaps predict, those who might engage in trust betrayal.

We sought and obtained cooperation from over 2,000 police departments nationwide. Sixty-nine of those departments had the type of cases we were interested in and were able to supply all of the personality, background and offense data we required. Complete data sets were obtained on 439 offenders and 439 matched non-offenders. . . .

Background of the study

The primary purpose of this study was to determine the feasibility of screening for police corruption using currently administered psychological instruments. Scales and items from four psychological tests actually administered to the subjects as part of their standard pre-employment screening process were utilized. Those tests were the Minnesota Multiphasic Personality Inventory (MMPI), the California Personality Inventory (CPI), the 16 Personality Factor Questionnaire (16PF), and the Inwald Personality Inventory (IPI). The goal was to identify those sets of items and scales that could differentiate officers who engaged in corrupt acts after they were hired *from* an equal number of matched officers presumed not to have engaged in acts of corruption. Violators were a) identified by their department as having engaged in at least one act of corruption, b) had their involvement in that act corroborated/substantiated, and c) were formally punished for committing that violation.

Over 4,000 departments were contacted and asked whether they were both willing and able to participate in this study. A vast majority of the departments that responded either did not a) administer psychological pre-employment tests, b) retain or have access to the results of those previously administered tests, or c) have a current or former officer that they successfully caught and punished for corruption. Sixty-nine departments met all of the prerequisites and supplied personality test data on 878 officers (439 violators and 439 non-violators). All of the officers included in the study were anonymous.

The pre-employment personality test most frequently administered to those officers when they originally applied to their respective departments was the MMPI (92.7%), followed by CPI (41.0%), 16PF (11.2%) and IPI (11.0%). Many of the subjects completed more than one of those psychological tests during their selection phase.

Two-thirds of the subject data was placed in a developmental sub-sample. This sub-sample was used to try to identify or create scales that predicted corruption. The other third of the cases was used as a "hold-out" sample to cross-validate those findings.

The study's results

Overall, the predictive scales did very poorly during the attempted cross-validation. This indicates that at best only modest improvements in combating corruption can be made through better utilization of the personality data that is being collected. Of the few personality measures that had any success in the cross-validation attempts, they tended to indicate that the violators had *more*

- difficulty getting along with others,
- delinquent histories, and
- indications of maladjustment, immaturity, irresponsibility, and/or unreliability.

Non-violators, on-the-other-hand, tended to be *more*

- tolerant of others,
- willing and able to maintain long-term positive relationships with others,
- willing to accept responsibility and blame, and/or
- controlled by guilt and remorse.

Violators also appeared somewhat *less* willing to respond in a manner that might reflect negatively upon themselves (which they probably thought would lower their chances of being hired). Suggestions are made for developing a Forthcomingness scale to be able to better control for this effect.

Examining the data

The lower than anticipated relationship between the personality measures and later acts of corruption was probably due to several factors. Environmental factors undoubtedly played a key role in affecting the outcome, such as whether the officer a) was assigned to work with a supervisor, partner or training officer who was corrupt; b) worked in a department or community where offering and accepting bribes is commonplace; c) was assigned to work in high corruption prone duties or areas; and/or d) had suffered personal set-backs that might make that officer more vulnerable to temptation. However, those factors should have also affected the outcome of other corruption and betrayal of trust studies. Some of the effects of personality would have been attenuated by some of the police applicants with certain personality-related problems being screened out as a result of psychological testing or other components of the background investigation. However, it is not anticipated that corrections for range restriction caused by that prior screening will substantially affect the results, especially if corrections for true base-rate are also applied. The primary differences between this study and those that have found much higher correlations in the past appear to be:

1) this study was based on the actual pre-employment tests completed by subjects at the time they were applying for their position,

2) the subjects were probably motivated to hide past problems and issues during the psychological testing phase *as opposed to* prisoner-
based studies where subjects may be motivated to reveal or exaggerate their past problems,

3) all of the subjects actively sought law enforcement positions and
probably knew prior to applying for those positions that one of the
selection requirements that would be imposed was passing a thorough background investigation,

4) the findings reflect the extent to which police pre-employment
personality test information predicts subsequent acts of corruption
as opposed to those in prisoner-based studies which reflect the extent to which personality test information differentiates convicted
prisoners from a selected group of non-prisoners who have been
asked to take part in a study, and

5) the effects of chance were better controlled for than in many other
studies through use of larger samples, multiple test versions measuring the same constructs, and use of a hold-out sample.

The single best predictor of corruption found in this study was not a
personality measure. It was post-hire misconduct. Officers who got into
trouble with their supervisors for volitional acts of misconduct were signifi-
cantly more likely to be punished for later engaging in acts of corruption. . . .

Major findings of the study

Substantial improvements in reducing police corruption and other acts of
trust betrayal do not appear possible solely through improved utilization
of the personality factors currently measured by most police departments.
The decision of whether or not to engage in acts of corruption is shaped
to a great extent by environmental factors and foreground triggers. Those
factors and triggers are often not associated with the employee's personality. The low correlations found between personality and corruption indicate that only very modest improvements can be made through better
utilization of the personality data that are already being collected.

Undoubtedly, some of the strength of the relationship between corruption and personality was reduced in this study because those same
personality measures, as well as other background screening procedures,
were already being used by the departments to help screen candidates.
The data from this study will be made available to other researchers, and
corrections for range restriction can be applied by those possessing the
necessary police applicant normative data on the personality measures.
Even with those corrections it is unlikely that the amount of variance ac-
counted for by the personality measures will raise substantially. This
means that it is unlikely that improved personality screening has the potential to substantially reduce police corruption. Rather, it appears that
significant reductions in corruption will only be possible if the resulting
knowledge of the personality factors affecting corruption is combined
with systematic efforts to reduce the environmental factors and foreground triggers that also contribute to its occurrence.

It has been noted that a challenge to modern policing is not eradi-
cating corruption but rather maintaining vigilance and attention to the
issue such that when the precursors of corruption emerge appropriate

measures will be taken to control them. This study sought to leverage a selection procedure already in place in many departments (i.e., screening candidates with psychological tests) to create a reliable, valid, ethically responsible and legally defensible means to decrease the level of corruption experienced by departments.

The leveraging approach that was utilized sought to find scales and items on certain psychological tests (the MMPI, CPI, 16PF and IPI) that differentiated individuals who had betrayed the public trust from those that had not. What was discovered is that the best predictor of violator status assessed by this study was an officer's history of on-the-job acts of misconduct, not personality measures.

Although the personality measures were not as strong predictors as anticipated, certain personality characteristics were found that appear to be related to violator status. In this study, . . . violators are more likely to have a history of disregarding or expressing disregard for the rules and laws that govern society, as well as for the individuals responsible for enforcing them. Additionally, . . . scores suggest that violators may frequently be described as immature, unreliable, and irresponsible. . . . Violators may be overly concerned about how they appear to others on the surface. Violators . . . indicate that they are also less likely to divulge attitudes and behaviors that they feel might harm their chances of being selected for the law enforcement positions for which they were applying. However, the violators did respond affirmatively more often to delinquency-related items, such as "I have been in trouble with the law" and "I have been suspended from school.". . .

Although the personality measures were not as strong predictors as anticipated, certain personality characteristics were found that appear to be related to violator status.

The non-violators are more likely to be described as tolerant of others, thoughtful concerning their relationships with others, achievement oriented, and willing to accept responsibility for their actions. The findings . . . also suggest that non-violators are more affected by internal behavioral controls such as guilt and remorse.

Not only can these traits be assessed to some degree by personality tests, they can also be addressed by questions asked during subject interviews and during the employment and reference checks conducted as part of background investigations.

To summarize, police officers who betrayed the public trust were more likely to have engaged in post-hire acts of workplace misconduct than non-violators. Further, while background investigation data on the subjects was not collected, the violator's item responses and scale scores on the personality tests indicate that they were also more likely to have engaged in delinquent acts in other settings (e.g., high school). Non-violators, on-the-other-hand, appear to be more concerned about behaving in a socially responsible manner, as well as maintaining stable interpersonal relationships with friends, family, coworkers, and supervisors.

Organizations to Contact

The editors have compiled the following list of organizations concerned with the issues debated in this book. The descriptions are derived from materials provided by the organizations. All have publications or information available for interested readers. The list was compiled on the date of publication of the present volume; the information provided here may change. Be aware that many organizations take several weeks or longer to respond to inquiries, so allow as much time as possible.

Fraternal Order of Police (FOP)
1410 Donelson Pike, Suite A-17, Nashville, TN 37217
(615) 399-0900 • fax: (615) 399-0400
website: www.grandlodgefop.org

The FOP is the world's largest union for sworn law enforcement officers. The organization represents police officers in grievances against their departments and protects the rights of officers who are accused of crimes. The FOP publishes the quarterly *FOP Journal*, which covers all aspects of law enforcement duty and occasionally discusses issues concerning corruption and misconduct.

International Association of Chiefs of Police
515 N. Washington St., Alexandria, VA 22314
(703) 836-6767 • (800) THE IACP • fax: (703) 836-4543
website: www.theiacp.org

The association consists of police executives who provide consultation and research services to, and support educational programs for, police departments nationwide. The association publishes the monthly magazine *Police Chief*, which covers all aspects of law enforcement duty, and the report "Police Accountability and Citizen Review."

National Association for the Advancement of Colored People (NAACP)
4805 Mt. Hope Dr., Baltimore, MD 21215-3297
(410) 358-8900 • fax: (410) 358-3818 • information hot line: (410) 521-4939
website: www.naacp.org

The NAACP is a civil rights organization that works to end racial discrimination in America. It researches and documents police brutality and provides legal services for victims of brutality and racial profiling. The NAACP publishes the book *Beyond the Rodney King Story: An Investigation of Police Misconduct in Minority Communities* and the magazine *Crisis* ten times per year.

National Institute of Justice (NIJ)
National Criminal Justice Reference Service (NCJRS)
PO Box 6000, Rockville, MD 20850
(800) 851-3420 • (301) 519-5500
e-mail: askncjrs@ncjrs.org • website: www.ojp.usdoj.gov/nij

A component of the Office of Justice Programs of the U.S. Department of Justice, NIJ supports and conducts research on crime, criminal behavior, and crime prevention. NCJRS acts as a clearinghouse for criminal justice information for researchers and other interested individuals. It publishes and distributes *Police Integrity: Public Service with Honor.*

National Organization of Black Law Enforcement Executives (NOBLE)
4609 Pinecrest Office Park Dr., Suite F, Alexandria, VA 22312-1442
(703) 658-1529 • fax: (703) 658-9479
e-mail: noble@noblenatl.org • website: www.noblenatl.org

NOBLE serves the interests of black law enforcement officials. It works to eliminate racism, increase minority participation at all levels of law enforcement, and foster community involvement in working to reduce urban crime and violence. NOBLE recommends policies to ensure police officers are held accountable for their actions and have uncompromising integrity. Its publications include the quarterly magazine *NOBLE National* and the newsletter *NOBLE Actions.*

October 22nd Coalition
c/o KHL, Inc., PO Box 124, 160 First Ave., New York, NY 10009
(888) No-Brutality • NYC: (212) 822-8596 • Chicago: (773) 794-8114
e-mail: oct22@unstoppable.com • website: www.unstoppable.com/22

The coalition is a diverse group of activist organizations and individuals concerned about police brutality. October 22nd is the date of the coalition's annual "National Day of Protest Against Police Brutality, Repression, and the Criminalization of a Generation," which is intended to raise awareness about police misconduct. The coalition publishes a newsletter, available on-line, as part of its efforts to organize protest activities. It also coordinates the Stolen Lives Project, a report that documents the names of those who have been brutalized and killed by the police since 1990.

People Against Racial Terror (PART)
PO Box 1055, Culver City, CA 90232
(310) 288-5003
e-mail: part2001@usa.net
website: www.geocities.com/CapitolHill/Lobby/4801

PART believes that police abuse, brutality, and corruption are widespread problems that demand immediate national attention. PART views the police as an occupying army in oppressed communities, and it believes community monitoring of police is the best way to prevent incidents of police harassment and violence. In addition to books and videos, PART publishes *Turning the Tide: Journal of Anti-Racist Activism, Research, and Education.*

Police Executive Research Forum (PERF)
1120 Connecticut Ave. NW, Suite 930, Washington, DC 20036
(202) 466-7820
website: www.policeforum.org

PERF is a national professional association of police executives that seeks to increase public understanding of and stimulate debate on important criminal justice issues. PERF's numerous publications include the book *And Justice for All: Understanding and Controlling Police Abuse of Force* and the report "Racially Biased Policing: A Principled Response."

Police Foundation
1201 Connecticut Ave. NW, Suite 200, Washington, DC 20036
(202) 833-1460 • fax: (202) 659-9149
e-mail: pfinfo@policefoundation.org

The foundation conducts research projects on police practices and aims to improve the quality of police personnel. It publishes the report *Officer Behavior in Police-Citizen Encounters: A Descriptive Model and Implications for Less-than-Lethal Alternatives,* the paper *Policing for People,* and the monograph *Integrity for a Community Policing Environment.*

Bibliography

Books

Anthony V. Bouza	*Police Unbound: Corruption, Abuse, and Heroism by the Boys in Blue.* Amherst, NY: Prometheus, 2001.
William J. Bratton with Peter Knobler	*Turnaround: How America's Top Cop Reversed the Crime Epidemic.* New York: Random House, 1998.
Marcia R. Chaiken	*Kids, Cops, and Communities.* Washington, DC: U.S. Department of Justice, 1998.
Dean J. Champion	*Police Misconduct in America: A Reference Handbook.* Santa Barbara, CA: ABC-CLIO, 2001.
Gabriel J. Chin, ed.	*New York City Police Corruption Investigation Commissions, 1894–1994.* Buffalo, NY: W.S. Hein, 1997.
Ted Gottfried	*Police Under Fire.* Brookfield, CT: Twenty-First Century Books, 1999.
Robert Jackall	*Wild Cowboys: Urban Marauders and the Forces of Order.* Cambridge, MA: Harvard University Press, 1997.
Gerald E. Kelly	*Honor for Sale: The Darkest Chapter in the History of New York's Finest.* New York: Sharon, 1999.
John Kleinig	*The Ethics of Policing.* Cambridge, MA: Cambridge University Press, 1996.
James Lardner	*Crusader: The Hell-Raising Police Career of Detective David Durk.* New York: Random House, 1996.
Rickey D. Lashley	*Policework: The Need for a Noble Character.* Westport, CT: Praeger, 1995.
Richard C. Lindberg	*To Serve and Collect: Chicago Politics and Police Corruption from the Lager Beer Riot to the Summerdale Scandal: 1855–1960.* Carbondale: Southern Illinois University Press, 1998.
Stephen Mastrofski	*Community Policing in Action: Lessons from an Observational Study.* Washington, DC: U.S. Department of Justice, 1998.
R.I. Mawby	*Policing Across the World: Issues for the Twenty-First Century.* London: UCL Press, 1999.
Frank McKetta	*Police, Politics, Corruption: The Mixture Dangerous to Freedom and Justice.* Camp Hill, PA: Polis, 2000.
Larry McShane	*Cops Under Fire: The Reign of Terror Against Hero Cops.* Washington, DC: Regnery, 1999.

Val Nadin   *Breaking the Blue Line: A Dying Declaration.* New York: Vantage Press, 1998.

National Institute of   *Police Integrity: Public Service with Honor.* Washington,
Justice and Office of   DC: U.S. Department of Justice, 1997.
Community Oriented
Policing Services

New York   *Performance Study: A Follow-Up Review of the Internal*
Commission to   *Affairs Bureau Command Center.* New York: The
Combat Police   Commission, 1999.
Corruption

New York   *A Review of the New York City Police Department's Methods*
Commission to   *for Gathering Corruption-Related Intelligence.* New York:
Combat Police   The Commission, 1999.
Corruption

Michael J. Palmiotto,   *Police Misconduct: A Reader for the Twenty-First Century.*
ed.   Upper Saddle River, NJ: Prentice-Hall, 2001.

Jeff Slowikowski and   *Community Policing and Youth.* Washington, DC: U.S.
Helen Connelling   Department of Justice, 1999.

Randall Sullivan   *Labyrinth: A Detective Investigates the Murders of Tupac Shakur and Biggie Smalls, the Implication of Death Row Records' Suge Knight, and the Origins of the Los Angeles Police Scandal.* New York: Atlantic Monthly Press, 2002.

Periodicals

Susan Beck   "L.A. Confidential: Big-Firm Lawyers Tried to Fix the Los Angeles Police Department," *American Lawyer*, June 2000.

Angela Bonavoglia   "Breaking the Blue Wall of Silence," *Ms.*, January/February 1997.

Erwin Chemerinsky   *An Independent Analysis of the Los Angeles Police Department's Board of Inquiry Report on the Rampart Scandal,* no date.

John Cloud   "L.A. Confidential, for Real," *Time*, September 27, 1999.

Adam Cohen   "Police Line: Do Not Cross: Gangsta Cops," *Time*, March 6, 2000.

Tessa DeCarlo   "Why Women Make Better Cops," *Glamour*, September 1995.

Economist   "When Sheriffs Go Wrong: Georgia's Worst Sheriffs," February 17, 2001.

Ana Figueroa   "O.J.'s New Defense," *Newsweek*, February 28, 2000.

Donna Foote and   "'Time and Again, I Stepped Over the Line,'" *Newsweek*,
Ana Figueroa   March 6, 2000.

Dianne Freely and   "Organizing for Accountability," *Against the Current*,
David Finkel   November/December 1999.

Gilbert G. Gallegos   "Cops Targeted Unfairly," *FOP Journal*, January 2001. Available from www.grandlodgefop.org.

Ken Hamblin — "Police Used as Fall Guys in Fight Against Crime," *Conservative Chronicle*, December 27, 1995. Available from PO Box 37077, Boone, IA 50037-0077.

Noelle Howey — "Good Women, Bad Cops," *Mademoiselle*, October 1999.

William F. Jasper — "Local Police Under Siege," *New American*, May 11, 1998. Available from 770 Westhill Blvd., Appleton, WI 54914.

David Kocieniewski — "System of Policing the Police Is Attacked from Without and Within," *New York Times*, December 19, 1997.

James Lardner — "A Mythical Blue Wall of Silence," *U.S. News & World Report*, September 1, 1997.

Los Angeles Police Department — *Board of Inquiry in the Rampart Area Corruption Incident*, March 1, 2000. Available from www.lapd.org.

Jack Maple — "Police Must Be Held Accountable," *Newsweek*, June 21, 1999.

Terry McCarthy — "L.A. Gangs Are Back," *Time*, September 3, 2001.

Salim Muwakkil — "No Cop Accountability," *In These Times*, April 11, 1999.

Arch Puddington — "The War on the War on Crime," *Commentary*, May 1999.

Barbara Reynolds — "Our Sons Under Siege," *Essence*, November 1999.

Carl T. Rowan — "The Lawless Lawmen of Our Nation's Capital," *New Republic*, January 19, 1998.

Alicia C. Shepard — "Taking Down the Sheriff," *American Journalism Review*, July/August 1998.

Richard Stratton — "The Making of Bonecrusher," *Esquire*, September 1999.

Peg Tyre — "Betrayed by a Badge," *Newsweek*, June 18, 2001.

Ann Scott Tyson — "Moves to Police the Police Gain Ground," *Christian Science Monitor*, November 13, 1996.

Jack E. White — "The White Wall of Silence," *Time*, June 7, 1999.

Richard Wolkomir — "Protect and Serve," *Smithsonian*, November 1998.

Index

Giuliani, Rudolph W., 39

Hoke, Mike, 53
Hoover administration, 77

integrity
 codes of, management fails to enforce,
  50–51
 core virtues relating to, 14–15
 measurement of, 16–17
 psychological types lacking in, 13–14
 teaching of, 16

Johns Hopkins Police Executive
 Leadership Program, 15–16
Johnson, Samuel, 10

Kelly, Raymond, 56
King, Rodney, 27
 see also Rodney King beating
Kleinig, John, 20
Klockars, Carl, 32
Knapp Commission, 28, 42
 on police training, 49–50
 on types of corruption, 45

Lee, Bill Lann, 30
Lexow committee, 77
Los Angeles Police Department, 79
 corruption in, 55, 77–79
 low esteem of, 62
 Rampart scandal, 7–9, 31, 35–36, 60,
  63–64, 80
 perjury in, 57, 58, 59

Martinez, Al, 60
maturity
 as factor in drug-related corruption,
  47, 48–49
McNamara, Joseph D., 33, 54
Miranda warning
 given to police, 37
Mitchell, Margaret, 61
Mollen, Milton, 40
Mollen Commission, 39
 on motives for drug-related
  corruption, 40, 45–46
 on police brutality, 51
 on police culture and training, 49–50
 on police supervision, 49–50
 on types of corruption, 44–45
Monkkonen, Eric, 75
Morgenthau, Robert, 59
motives for corruption
 drug-related, 45–46
Murphy, Patrick, 19

neighborhood ties
 as factor in drug-related corruption, 51

Nelson, Jack, 53
Newburn, Tim, 21, 22
New Orleans Police Department, 55–56
New York City Commission to Combat
 Police Corruption, 39
Nodal, Adolfo V., 68

O.J. Simpson case, 59, 64–65
Omnibus Crime Control and Safe Streets
 Act of 1968, 72
opportunity
 as factor in drug-related corruption,
  47, 48
Ovando, Javier Francisco, 7

Parker, William H., 78
Parks, Bernard C., 8, 64
Perez, Rafael, 7, 8, 35–36, 61, 62
perjury
 extent of, is exaggerated, 64
 police often commit, to convict guilty,
  34, 57–59, 76
Perry, Frank L., 18
Plato, 10, 11
police departments
 are difficult to reform, 75–78
 federal oversight of, has reduced
  misconduct, 70–74
police officers
 acculturation of, 26–28
 are pressured to be corrupt, 30–32
 corrupt, as heroes, 66–69
 cynicism among, 25–26
 killings of, 62
 public confidence in, 12
political corruption, 75–76
predatory crime
 by police, 35
Punch, M., 22

Rampart division, 67–68
Rampart scandal (LAPD), 7–9, 31, 35–36,
 60, 63–64, 80
 perjury in, 57, 58, 59
Rangel, Charles B., 38
reform
 areas in need of, 71
 is difficult for police departments,
  75–78
Reno, Janet, 70, 74
Republic (Plato), 11
Richardson, James, 77
Rodney King beating, 55, 62, 64, 72, 76
Rosenbaum, Steven H., 70

Samarra, Ed, 55
Sarabyn, Kelly, 79
Serpico, Frank, 27
Shaw, Frank L., 77–78